浙江省普通高校“十三五”新形态教材

# 高职国际交流英语教程


主　编　缪　莉　金忍冬

副主编　张　俏

参　编　张　梅　袁相科　张华丽　项　敏
朱晓洁　吴　倩　刘　励

北京理工大学出版社
BEIJING INSTITUTE OF TECHNOLOGY PRESS

## 内 容 简 介

本教材分为五大主题:海外院校、交通出行、旅游出境、购物与饮食、求职应聘,每个主题下细分成不同的技能点,形成29个独立的单元知识点。单元知识点的设计秉承“项目式”教学理念,内容融合语言技能和社会技能的学习。教学流程上顺应“互联网+教育”的理念,探索翻转课堂授课模式,突出课前自学环节,加强课内师生互动。通过本教材的学习,学生不仅能够拓宽国际化视野、增强海外学习生活以及信息技术应用的能力,又能够在潜移默化中提高解决问题的能力、沟通能力和学习能力等一系列的关键能力。



**图书在版编目(CIP)数据**

高职国际交流英语教程/缪莉,金忍冬主编.—北京:北京理工大学出版社,2019.8 (2022.1重印)

ISBN 978-7-5682-7400-5

Ⅰ.①高… Ⅱ.①缪… ②金… Ⅲ.①英语-高等职业教育-教材 Ⅳ.①H319.39

中国版本图书馆CIP数据核字(2019)第174505号

出版发行/北京理工大学出版社有限责任公司
社　　址/北京市海淀区中关村南大街5号
邮　　编/100081
电　　话/(010)68914775(总编室)
(010)82562903(教材售后服务热线)
(010)68944723(其他图书服务热线)
网　　址/http://www.bitpress.com.cn
经　　销/全国各地新华书店
印　　刷/北京虎彩文化传播有限公司
开　　本/710毫米×1000毫米 1/16
印　　张/10
字　　数/195千字
版　　次/2019年8月第1版 2022年1月第3次印刷
定　　价/39.80元

责任编辑/武丽娟
文案编辑/武丽娟
责任校对/刘亚男
责任印制/施胜娟

图书出现印装质量问题,请拨打售后服务热线,本社负责调换

# 前 言

很多学生学了多年的英语，是不是还会有这样的困惑：在课堂上学英语时既看得懂，也说得出，基础好的学生甚至跨过了层层英语考试的门槛，但是当真正去到海外学习生活时，大部分的学生都是一片茫然，仿佛所学的此英语非彼英语。出现这种情况的原因主要有三个方面：一是我们从小到大英语教材的培养目标主要集中在英语听说读写等语言技能的培养上，但是语言应用是一个综合能力，它不仅涉及语言知识和技能本身，还需要语言以外的知识、技能、策略、认知、情感等的综合应用，因此学生由于缺乏海外学习生活的机会，只能在真空的象牙塔里学习纯语言技能；二是我们从小到大的英语教材在设计时就考虑到不同层次的语言学习者的词汇学习难度，会对语言材料进行简化或者碎片化处理，换言之，我们过往学习的语言材料是经过加工的，语言材料的真实性会流失很多，因此当我们真正接触到真实语言材料时会有陌生感；三是许多同学缺乏国际交流的途径，也不会使用现代化信息技术来助力外语学习，因此对海外学习生活的环境认知极少。殊不知语言学习，最重要的是文化背景、社会常识的认知。

针对以上问题，本教材在学习材料的选择上将真实性和应用性放在首要位置来讲。教材的文本内容全部取自英文官方网页以及专栏文章。技能知识点的设计来自团队教师丰富的海外学习生活经验的提炼。教材配套的视频案例内容全部引用最真实的英文资料，学生可以跟随教师的讲解在实景中直接输入原汁原味的语言信息。实际上，与学习生活相关的英文网页的文字难度并不大。对于部分不认识的生词，教师鼓励学生采用现代化的信息技术进行翻译。由于将互联网的应用引入了语言学习，学生可以突破地域限制、语言能力的限制，所以在一定程度上拉近了与世界的距离，也使语言学习有了真实感。综上所述，本教材的着力点不在于听说读写的语法知识，而在于通过传授解决实际问题的社会技能来推进语言技能的自然习得。

本教材以培养学生的英语实际应用能力为目标，以网络时代下信息技术的应用为切入点，教授学生如何利用信息工具解决海外学习、生活中遇到的实际问题。通过本教材的学习，学生不仅能够拓宽国际化视野、增强海外学习生活以及信息技术应用的能力，还能够在潜移默化中提高解决问题的能力、沟通能力、学习能力等一系列的关键能力。

教材内容分为五大主题：海外院校、交通出行、旅游出境、购物与饮食、求职应聘。每个主题下细分成不同的技能点，形成 29 个独立的单元知识点。每个单元知识点的设计秉承“项目式”教学理念，融合语言技能和社会技能的学习。

在知识点的设计流程上顺应“互联网+教育”的理念，探索翻转课堂授课模式，突出课前自学环节，加强课上师生互动。单元内容编排为课前学习和课上学习两大部分。课前学习（Pre - class Learning）分为话题热身（Topic）、小测试（Test），以及视频内相关单词的学习（Wordlist）3个部分。特别提醒的是Test里的问题针对视频内容设置，用来检测学生的预习效果。第二部分课上学习（In - class Learning）分为技能知识点（Skill Tips）的提炼、相关话题的拓展阅读（Reading Text）以及课堂上的项目实操（Project）3个部分。教师在课上主要是以活动的组织者、协调者的身份来展开相关技能的任务训练。

本教材搭配使用的视频内容由浙江省在线精品课程《国际交流英语互联网指南》提供。希望本教材能够教授学生最实际的海外学习生活技能。由于编者水平有限，教材中如有疏漏和其他不尽完善之处，恳请广大读者提出宝贵意见与建议。

编　者

# 目　　录

# Unit 1 Oversea College

Learning Objectives

You are going to learn the following skills that are necessary for your study at abroad, not only for your application but also for your campus living.

- ➢ You will have an overview of oversea colleges.
- ➢ You will experience the orientation week of oversea colleges.
- ➢ You will learn to find the key information on the college websites.
- ➢ You will learn to apply for on – campus housing.
- ➢ You will learn to write an enquiry letter online.
- ➢ You will learn to telephone the University for Consultation.

## 1. The Overview of Oversea College

**Pre - class Learning:** Watch the video and have the overview of oversea college, then finish the following tasks.

**Topic:** Think about it and share your opinions on the online forum.

1. Do you have the ideal oversea university?
   (cues: ivy league, top 100, TAFE, etc.)
2. What is your general impression on the oversea university?
   (cues: diverse students, academic life, multiple clubs, international fame, energetic community, unique experience, world - class professor, etc.)

**Test:** Please watch the video online and answer the questions in the form.

| Please answer the following questions according to what you have learned from the video. |
|---|
| 1. How many academic years does it take to get a bachelor's degree in the United States? |
| 2. Do American students have to decide their majors at the first year in the university? |
| 3. If some students don't have plenty of time to study, what kind of study will fit them well? |
| 4. If you only have the certificate now, do you have the possibility to get the university degree in the future? |

### Wordlist

Glossary

| | | | |
|---|---|---|---|
| public university | 公立大学 | private university | 私立大学 |
| community university | 社区大学 | sponsor | 资助 |
| tuition fee | 学费 | scholarship | 奖学金 |
| general education | 通识教育 | major course | 专业课 |
| core course | 核心课 | general course | 通识课 |

续表

| bachelor degree | 学士学位 | certificate | 证书 |
|---|---|---|---|
| diploma | 文凭 | undergraduate | 本科 |
| postgraduate | 研究生 | master | 硕士 |
| credit | 学分 | short - term training | 短期培训 |

## In - class Learning

### Skill Tips

*Knowledge about western educational system*

- Types of colleges/universities in the USA: Public University / Private University / Community University
- Different study level: Undergraduate / Postgraduate / Tertiary / Short - term training; Degree: Bachelor / Master / Doctor / Certificate (no degree)
- Credit system: compulsory course, elective course, core course, major course, etc.

### Reading Text

Study Abroad in College——benefits & challenges

Studying abroad offers a unique opportunity to grow academically, professionally, and personally while going on an adventure. There are a number of other benefits to study abroad; however, there are also numerous challenges. Consider the pros and cons, and decide if studying abroad may be right for you.

*Benefits*

1. Experience a Foreign Culture

Visiting foreign lands in person is an entirely different experience. When you study abroad, you participate in the day – to – day life of a new locale, gaining a first – hand understanding and new appreciation of the culture.

2. Improve Your Second Language Skills

You may already be fluent in a second language, or you might study abroad in one of the many countries where English is spoken as a first language.

3. Explore Your Own Heritage

Students whose familial heritage stems from abroad will often choose to explore their ethnicity and ancestry. In fact, reports show that minority students benefit both personally and academically when they have studied abroad in the country of their family's origin.

4. Learn How to Communicate Across Cultures

Studying abroad helps you become familiar with the customs and traditions of the country in which you are studying, in addition to the language. By interacting with locals, you can develop an appreciation for the culture and its differences from your own.

5. Become More Independent

Studying abroad removes you from the normal support network that you are accustomed to back home. While on the other hand, being away from friends and family can seem daunting, it is also a chance for you to hone your own skills and gain some independence.

*Challenges*

1. Homesickness Can Occur Frequently

If you have never spent much time far from home, this could be a serious issue. You may find yourself yearning for the people you left back home, and the less outgoing you are, the more of a problem this can become.

2. It May Be Difficult to Get to Know Locals

In some countries, the locals will be warm and inviting, while in others, it might take a little more effort to make friends. If you're concerned, find out in advance how Americans are typically received and treated in the area.

3. You May Experience Culture Shock When You Return Home

Once you become used to a foreign environment, your home might actually seem foreign to you. This effect will be most notable when returning from countries where cultural differences from your home are numerous.

(adapted from website https://www. moneycrashers. com/reasons – why – study – abroad – benefits/)

Question 1: How do minority students explore their own heritage?

Question 2: By which way can students develop their understanding of foreign cultures and their own culture?

Question 3: What type of people may suffer from homesickness more?

Question 4: What does "culture shock" mean from the text?

## Project

Let us do the discussion on what we have learned from the class. Follow the steps.

Step 1: Use the information from the above text and give a short talk about your personal understanding of what you will get from the oversea university.

> Sample structure
> From what I've learned in this class, I know there are challenges and benefits when we study at abroad.
> What benefits are...
> What challenges are...

________________________________________

________________________________________

________________________________________

________________________________________

Step 2: Try to compare the eastern and western universities and list their commons and differences as much as possible.

> Sample structure
> Both in eastern and western universities, we have to...
> However, in eastern universities, they..., while in the west, they...

________________________________________

________________________________________

________________________________________

________________________________________

## 2. Orientation Week

**Pre - class Learning**: Watch the video and have the overview of the orientation week, then finish the following tasks.

**Topic**: Think about it and share your opinions on the online forum.

1. What is your first week impression on your college life?
   (cues: enrollment, faculty, upperclassmen, dormitory, etc.)
2. What is your most concern when entering into a new college?
   (cues: dormitory, course, teacher, food, etc. )

**Test**: Please watch the video online and answer the questions in the form.

| Please answer the following questions according to what you have learned from the video. |
|---|
| 1. What does orientation week mean? |
| 2. How long is the orientation week? |
| 3. What should international students do during orientation week? |
| 4. If you have some security problem, what should you do? |

### Wordlist

Glossary

| | | | |
|---|---|---|---|
| orientation | 适应，情况介绍 | register | 注册 |
| induction | 入门培训，就职仪式 | information session | 宣讲会 |
| access | 进入 | counselling | 辅导 |
| campus security | 校园安全 | financial support | 财政支持 |

## In – class Learning

### Skill Tips

*Advice for Orientation week*

• Upload your orientation schedule: various programs, activities, tours launched in orientation week

• Access your online – system: oversea students use their uni – account to receive and deliver all messages with college

• Connect to your free Wi – Fi: free Wi – Fi is available all around the campus

• Sort out your student card: student cards could be used in many places around the campus

• Checkout your details: update your personal information

• Locate your support service: clinic, financial support, student center, accommodation, counselling office, etc.

• Campus security: remember emergency phone number

*How to break ice when you first meet someone*

• Smile, handshake, bow

• Appreciation, praise

• Talk about common interests or hot news

• Self – introduction

### Reading Text

Student Club Spotlight: Overseas Travel Club

The Overseas Travel Club is one of the cultural and international clubs at Cazenovia College. It provides students with opportunities unlike any other club on campus. Students have the opportunity to travel overseas for week – long, life – changing

trips. Each year, the student club president and staff supervisor choose a destination for the upcoming academic year. Places selected include Australia, England, France, Greece, Ireland, and New Zealand. A group of students are currently travelling to Italy and the next destination is Spain.

This year's club presidents—Erin Willis, interior design senior, and Erin Grabosky, studio art junior—say the Overseas Travel Club pushes people to get out of their comfort zone. Travelling far, and often with a new group of people, can leave students feeling unsettled. Some club members are travelling for the first time. Students use the experience to broaden their cultural experiences and overcome anxieties, while making lifelong friends.

"Travelling long distances brings people together," says Willis. "I went into the club not knowing anyone and now I talk to its members every day."

Overseas Travel Club not only do students become close friends through the club, they also become experienced travelers and mentors for the first - time travelers in the club. Attributes of the Overseas Travel Club are that an individual can join anytime, and the trips are open not only to students, but also to the whole college community. In addition, it is not necessary to be a committed member of the club to take part in the trips, but club members do get the benefit of helping to choose future trips.

Students who want to take part in the club, but feel they cannot afford the trips can use club - sponsored fundraisers to help offset travel expenses. These fundraisers help students who need financial support to participate in a trip.

The Overseas Travel Club is the perfect club for anyone with the travel bug looking to experience a new country, or for students who have never traveled and want the experience in a safe, guided, group setting. Students looking to expand their horizons, meet like - minded individuals, and experience new cultures could benefit greatly from the Overseas Travel Club.

Students interested in the club or upcoming trips can email club presidents Erin

Willis (ecwillis@cazenovia.edu) or Erin Grabosky (ekgrabosky@cazenovia.edu). Club advisor HEOP Associate Director Sheila Marsh (smarsh@cazenovia.edu) is also available to answer questions.

(adapted from the website http://cazenovia.edu/news – and – events/news/student – club – spotlight – overseas – travel – club)

Question 1: What is the biggest difference between oversea travel club and other clubs?

Question 2: What is the benefit of travelling abroad for club members?

Question 3: If someone have financial problems, what should he/she do to join the trip?

Question 4: Who are available to answer questions?

## Project

Let us act out how we start a talk when we meet a new friend during the orientation week.

Step 1: Try to find out common interests with your foreign classmates. Or if you don't have foreign classmates, please imagine which common interests you will have. For example, clubs, food, courses, faculty, teachers, dormitory, etc.

Step 2: Suppose you are at the orientation week. You are starting a chat with other students at the faculty welcome party. Use strategies you have learned from the skills tips.

Model dialogue

A: Hi, I'm... (name), how are you?

B: Fine, thank you. I'm... (name). How are you?

A: I'm good. I'm from Shanghai and study marketing here.

B: It is great! Oh, What do you think of this party? Do you like it?

A: Yes. I like it. It is fantastic with so many tasty food and warm people.

B: Exactly!

Dialogue 1:

(substitute: name, hometown, opinion, etc.)

______________________________

______________________________

______________________________

______________________________

______________________________

## 3. College Website

**Pre - class Learning**: Watch the video and learn how to read English websites of the university, then finish the following tasks.

**Topic**: Think about it and share your opinions on the online forum.

1. How can you find information of oversea university?
   (cues: friends, news, websites, etc.)
2. Which contents on the university's websites will attract you most?
   (cues: courses, college introduction, transport, location, faculty, renowned professor, etc.)

**Test**: Please watch the video online and answer the questions in the form.

| Course details | |
|---|---|
| Faculty/University School: School of Architecture, Design and Planning | |
| Credit points required: 144 | Course abbreviation: BArchEnv |
| Usyd code: BPARCENV1000 | UAC code: 513100 |
| Study mode: On - campus day | Study type: UGCW |
| Location: Camperdown/Darlington campus | |
| Duration full time: 3 years full time for Domestic and International students | |
| Duration part time: None | |
| Please answer the following questions according to the information from the above chart.<br>1. How many credits does this course require?<br>2. Which school does this course belong to?<br>3. Does this course have part - time study mode? | |

### Wordlist

Glossary

| | | | |
|---|---|---|---|
| introduction | 介绍 | administrative office | 行政办公室 |
| campus | 校区 | event | 事件 |
| admission | 入学 | entry requirement | 入学要求 |

续表

| timeline | 时间轴 | qualification | 资格 |
|---|---|---|---|
| syllabus | 教学大纲 | annual | 每年 |
| status | 状态 | finance | 财政 |
| professor | 教授 | duration | 持续 |
| study mode | 学习方式 | faculty | 全体教员 |
| staff | 职员 | dean | 系主任 |

## In – class Learning

### Skill Tips

*Key information on college website*

The design of college websites may vary from one college to another college. But the main content is similarly distributed. If you have the ability to read the websites of oversea colleges, you may have the way to learn more details about a college.

*The main category of information on college website may be as follows*:

| *Study* | *Campus life* | *About college* |
|---|---|---|
| *course* | *accommodation* | *history, value* |
| *academic support* | *finances, fees, costs* | *campuses* |
| *admission* | *clubs and societies* | *governance, structure* |
| *finances, fees, costs* | *food, shops* | *faculties, communities* |
| *anything related to academic study* | *emergencies and personal safety* | *contact way* |
| | *health, wellbeing* | |
| | *maps and location* | |

## Reading Text

### College: What It's All About and Why It Matters

You might think that college is just high school continued, but it's not. College opens doors for you that high school doesn't. And college can change you and shape you in ways that you might not imagine.

*Become More Independent*

College work will challenge and inspire you. In college, you will:

- Explore subjects in greater depth than you did in high school
- Choose your own courses and class schedule
- Decide which extra curricular activities you'll focus on and how much time you'll give them

College helps students develop into mature, responsible and independent adults. But you're not entirely on your own: colleges offer students many kinds of help making this transition, such as tutoring and academic advising as well as counselling and other support.

*Explore Your Options*

One of the great things about being able to choose your own courses is that you get the opportunity to explore. You can try classes in a lot of different subjects, or you can dive right into a favorite subject. You may choose to begin training for a career right away. Or you may pick a major after taking some time to check out your options. Colleges offer classes and majors in subjects you've studied in high school—plus many more that you haven't.

*Explore Outside the Classroom*

College is about much more than just course work. A campus is its own world, and students have the chance to experience a wide range of activities. For example, college students may be able to:

- Publish newspapers
- Create TV and radio broadcasts
- Run their own government
- Stage performances
- Play sports
- Volunteer to improve their communities

*Invest in Yourself*

As you take on college work and participate in college life, you'll encounter new ideas and challenges. Along the way, you'll:

- Build knowledge, skills and brainpower
- Discover new passions
- Follow and satisfy your curiosity
- Learn more about yourself
- Bond with new friends
- Prepare for a future in which you're better equipped to give back

Whatever your destination, college can help you get there—even if you don't know where "there" is yet. Whether you've mapped out a long-term plan or you see new possibilities every day, college can help you become your future self.

(adapted from https://bigfuture.collegeboard.org/get-started/know-yourself/college-what-its-all-about-and-why-it-matters)

Question 1: From the author, does high school open doors for students?

Question 2: What should you do if you encounter problems in the process of being mature?

Question 3: What is the great thing to choose your own courses?

Question 4: Do college students have chances to volunteer to improve their community?

**Project**

Let us browse the website of Saint Martin's University together. Follow the steps.

Step 1: Visit https://www.stmartin.edu/, then click "Academics" and find "programs and schools", then pick the majors for undergraduate.

Step 2: Read an undergraduate academic catalog and answer the questions below.

1. Read Page 1 and tell us from which page we can find all the details of courses.

2. From Page 24 to 26, we can learn details of international undergraduate admission, can you tell us the different English language test requirements for international students?

3. From Page 46 to 49, we will know all fees charged at the university, like tuition fee, registration fees, health insurance, student services fees, etc. Please retell them in the class.

4. Choose one major that you are interested in from the catalog and tell us some course details of this major.

| Sample structure<br>I am interested in... (course name). I have learned this course... (general introduction of the course, credit required, syllabus, fees, etc.)<br>After graduation, we can work as... (career) |
| --- |

______________________________________________

______________________________________________

______________________________________________

______________________________________________

______________________________________________

## 4. On – campus Accommodation

**Pre – class Learning:** Watch the video and learn how to find on – campus accommodation, then finish the following tasks.

**Topic:** Think about it and share your opinions on the online forum.

1. When you choose an on – campus accommodation, which factors will affect your decision?
   (cues: room type, rate, facilities, secure environment, etc.)
2. What are the advantages and disadvantages of living on campus?
   (cues: close to teaching building, supportive community, continuous learning, etc.)

**Test:** Please watch the video online and answer the questions in the form.

Please translate the following expressions into Chinese.

1. first come, first serve ________________
2. single room with communal bathrooms ________________
3. self – catered ________________
4. resident ________________
5. unlimited Wi – Fi ________________
6. regular house keeping ________________
7. tutorial room ________________

### Wordlist

Glossary

| accommodation | 住宿 | eligibility | 资格 |
|---|---|---|---|
| facility | 设施 | balcony | 阳台 |
| applicant | 申请者 | gender | 性别 |
| room type | 房型 | male | 男性 |
| female | 女性 | residence hall | 学生宿舍 |
| kitchenette | 小厨房 | twin share room | 双人间 |

续表

| single room | 单人间 | in - house gym | 室内健身房 |
|---|---|---|---|
| cater | 提供饮食及服务 | fully - furnished | 全套家具 |
| lounge | 休息室 | house - keeping | 家政服务 |

## In - class Learning

### Skill Tips

*Knowledge about how to apply for student residence*

• Policy of student residence:

Many universities apply "first come, first serve" policy because not all universities have the capacity of accommodating all applicants. Therefore, students should apply for it as soon as they get the offer. However the policy of student residence may vary from one to one. You have to check it out when you apply for it online.

• Here are some factors for you to consider:

| *Eligibility* | *Fee* | *Room type* | *Facilities* | *Service* |
|---|---|---|---|---|
| *international/domestic student* | *room rate* | *single room, twin share room* | *unlimited Wi - Fi, TV, lounge* | *catered* |
| *study level* | *payment method* | *communal bathroom* | *library, tutorial room* | *self - catered* |
| *gender* | | *apartment, suite* | *in - house gym, music room* | *house - keeping* |

## Reading Text

### University Residence Halls

Your on – campus experience

As a resident in one of our halls, you can immerse yourself in campus life and also gain a sense of independence.

Our halls foster an intelligent, energetic community characterized by continuous learning. Funding is provided for students to run events and programs, so you can take advantage of the academic, social, athletic and cultural opportunities that surround you. Whether you'd like to take up fencing, learn to surf, manage a club or run tutorials, you'll find plenty of opportunities to get involved and learn new skills.

You will receive all the support you need with our residential advisers and live – in staff members running key programs in each hall to help support your health, well – being and academic progression. You can also speak to our central Accommodation Services Office about programs that will enable you to meet other students living on campus.

You can apply for university residence halls all year around, but note that most places are at capacity well before the academic year begins, so get in quick.

To apply, visit sydney. edu. au/accomodation.

*"The best part of living in the Queen Mary Building,*

*especially for an international student, is making friends.*

*Living on campus provides a great chance to conquer culture barriers."*

William Yang

Bachelor of Arts (Economics major)

Abercrombie Student Accommodation

Abercrombie is a lively community of 200 that fosters new experiences and enduring friendships. You'll have access to academic and well – being support as you progress through your studies.

Location

401 Abercrombie Street Darlington Campus

Rooms

– Studio apartment with kitchenette,

ensuite bathroom and study area

- Self – catered

Facilities and Inclusions

- Communal kitchen
- Common lounges
- Study and meeting rooms
- Outdoor terraces
- Extensive cultural, social, sporting and residence education programs
- Academic support network
- Student initiatives grant programs
- Student special interest groups

(adapted from usyd – accommodation – guide – 2018)

Question 1: If you need to get support for health, well – being and academic progression, who will you speak to?

Question 2: Do the university residence halls have the deadline for application?

Question 3: Does the Abercrombie Student Accommodation prepare three meals a day for residents?

Question 4: What is the best part of living on campus for the international students according to the commentary from the current students?

**Project**

Let us have a tour to Saint Martin's residence hall. Follow the steps.

Step 1: Visit website https://www.stmartin.edu/ and find "students' life". Then click "housing and dinning".

Step 2: You will find four types of residence halls, then pick one to click in.

Step 3: Suppose you are the staff in residence hall and try to introduce one type of these halls to the prospective students.

Directions: Please finish the above task as a group. Your presentation will include the eligibility of the housing type, amenities, specifications and rates, etc.

| Sample structure<br>I will choose … (hall name). This hall is for … (eligibility). The main type of this hall is …<br>It has … (amenities) and the room rate is … |
|---|

____________________________________________________________

____________________________________________________________

____________________________________________________________

# 5. Write an Enquiry Letter

**Pre – class Learning:** Watch the video and learn how to write an enquiry letter online, then finish the following tasks.

**Topic:** Think about it and share your opinions on the online forum.

1. In which circumstance will you write a letter to the university? And what questions will you ask?
   (cues: tuition fee, scholarship, dormitory, etc.)
2. What is a good enquiry letter?
   (cues: clear, short, concise, etc.)

**Test:** Please watch the video online and fill out the form below.

Please analyze the following letter and answer the questions as follows.
1. What is the purpose of this enquiry letter?
2. How many parts does this letter include and what are they?

Dear Sir/Madam,

I am a student from China and plan to learn English in Lancaster University for 6 months. Here are a few things I'd like to clarify.

Firstly, could you tell me how I can get to the university from my host home. Secondly, I'd like to know if I would have a separate room of my own. And I wonder if there are any children in the family. I would be beneficial to have someone of a similar age living with me. Also I tend to know if they have any special customs. Lastly, I wonder whether the fees should be paid monthly or weekly.

I look forward to hearing from you.

Yours sincerely

Li Hua

**Wordlist**

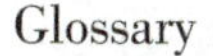

Glossary

| enquiry | 问询 | clarify | 弄清楚 |
|---|---|---|---|
| address | 称呼 | appreciate | 感谢 |

## In – class Learning

### Skill Tips

*Writing skills*

Pay attention to the format of an enquiry letter.

| Dear ×××, |
| --- |
| Paragraph 1: self – introduction, purpose of writing this letter |
| Paragraph 2: present the reason why you want to get this information, highlight the significance of the information |
| Paragraph 3: list the questions you want to ask |
| Paragraph 4: express your thanks and look forward to the reply |
| Yours sincerely |
| Name |

*Typical sentences used in an enquiry letter*

State purpose

- I'm writing to enquire about the details of …
- I am writing to ask that…

Ask for details

- Could you please tell me something about how to…
- I have several questions, as follows: 1、2、3、…
- I wonder if/whether you could tell me something about…
- I'd like to know something more about…

Express thanks

- I would be grateful to receive a prompt reply.
- I'd appreciate it very much if you could give me a reply.
- I am looking forward to your early reply.

### Reading Text

Methods of Communication

According to the Students Online: Global Trends report, released last week, email is by far the most popular method of communication with universities among prospective students. But depending on whether you have a quick query about your university application or a more involved question, there are a number of other methods of communication that can be used, ranging from social media messaging to printed letters.

1. Email

This method is both quicker than putting pen to paper and more formal than sending off a tweet. Students are sometimes dissatisfied with response times, but it is still the most popular method for those asking questions about applying to university.

2. Phone

Phone calls are the most immediate method of communication, and have the benefit of meaning you can get a more personal response to your enquiry—assuming you get through to the right person, and you're able to call during the university's office hours. Make sure you have a pen and paper ready to write down the information you're given, and be prepared to be put on hold.

3. Online contact form

Similar to sending an email but accessed via a form embedded in the university's website, online contact forms ensure that you provide all the relevant information about yourself along with your question. Response times may be slower, but you should eventually receive a reply, and often you'll be sent an email confirming that your query has been received and providing advice on when you should expect an answer.

4. Social media

Social media, such as the likes of Facebook and Twitter, is growing fast as a method of communication between students and university representatives, making it easier and faster for both to reach out. In some cases, large investments are being made by universities to improve these channels and to ensure a staff member is available to answer all queries within a short time. Using social media is often faster than other methods of communication, but may not be suitable for formal requests or highly specific questions.

(adapted from website page https://www.topuniversities.com/student-info/admissions-advice/university-application-queries-who-how-when-what-ask)

Question 1: Which method of communication is most popular with university among prospective students?

Question 2: What is the disadvantage of sending an email to university compared with phone calls?

Question 3: What advice does the author give when you enquire by phone calls?

Question 4: What is the advantage of using online contact form embedded in the university's website compared with sending emails?

**Project**

Let us write an enquiry letter to the university. Follow the steps.

Step 1: Translate Chinese into English.

1. 我写信是想询问国际学生如何才能拿到奖学金。

2. 我想询问一下你们的课程申请时间，因为我在网页上没有找到。

3. 我想知道贵校是否给国际学生提供住宿，如果有，是否要提早申请？

4. 如果能收到你的回信我将不胜感激。

5. 你能给我提供最新的招生简章吗？

Step 2: Visit website https://www.stmartin.edu/, and find email address from contact information of Saint Martin's university.

Step 3: Suppose you are a senior student in China and plan to study in the Saint Martin's university after graduation. But you are not sure about your eligibility to enter into Saint Martin's university. Please write an enquiry letter to the University and get some more information about the admission requirement or any other information you want to get.

Pay attention to your format of enquiry letter, and don't forget the basic elements required in the enquiry letter.

# 6. Make an Enquiry Call

**Pre – class Learning:** Watch the video and learn how to make a phone call to the university, then finish the following tasks.

**Topic:** Think about it and share your opinions on the online forum.

1. Do you know the ways to make an oversea phone call? What are they?
   (cues: face time, Skype, telecommunication preferential, etc. )
2. Can you tell us some etiquette of making a phone call?
   (cues: self – introduction, express thanks, leave the message, etc. )

**Test:** Please watch the video online and fill out the form at below.

Please answer the following questions according to what you have learned from the video.

1. What will you say when you pick up the phone?

2. What are common expressions when someone transfers you to the other line?

3. What is the suggestion from the video that will help you get clear information?

4. Can you say some telephone etiquette?

**Wordlist**

Glossary

| hold on | 等一下 | call back | 回电话 |
|---|---|---|---|
| hang on | 等一下 | pick up | 接电话 |
| put through | 连线 | get back to someone | 电话交还给某人 |
| get through | 连线 | switch off | 关机 |
| hang up | 挂电话 | cut off | 挂断 |

## In – class Learning

**Skill Tips**

*Something you have to know when you make a phone call*

- Check out the time when you make a phone: office hour, time zone.
- If you miss the information, don't hesitate to ask for repeat. Or you may prepare

a handy pen and paper and write down the things that you want to ask. It will help you release the tension.

*Expressions used in making a phone call*

| Content | The person is the one that you want to find | The person you want to find is not in at the moment | Transfer |
|---|---|---|---|
| Caller | Hello, this is ... (name).<br>I am calling to ...<br>May I speak to ... (name). | OK, I will call back later.<br>May I leave the message to him/her? | Thanks. |
| Person who answers the phone | Hello, this is ... (name).<br>Who is calling? | Sorry, he/she is not in at the moment.<br>Could you please call back later?<br>Could you mind leaving a message for her/him? | Hold on/hang on please.<br>I will transfer you to... (name).<br>Please hold the line, I will connect you to ... (name). |

## Reading Text

Important Phrases for English Telephone Conversations

Telephoning in English includes learning a number of special phrases, as well as focusing on listening skills. Some of the most important phrases include how to answer the phone, how to ask for others, how to connect, and how to take messages.

*Introducing Yourself*

Here are a few ways to informally introduce yourself on the telephone:

- This is Ken.
- Hello, Ken speaking.

If you'd like to reply more formally, use your full name.

- This is Jennifer Smith speaking.
- Hello, Jennifer Smith speaking.

If you are answering for a business, just state the business name. In this case, it's common to ask how you can help:

- Good morning, Thomson Company. How may I help you?

*British/American Difference*

- Hello, this is Ken.
- Brighton 0987654.

The first example response is in American English and the second is in British English.

In American English, we answer the phone stating "This is ...". In British English, it's common to answer the phone by stating the telephone number. The phrase "This is ..." is used only on the telephone to substitute the phrase "My name is ..." which is not used to answer the telephone.

*Asking Who Is on the Telephone*

Sometimes, you'll need to find out who is calling.

Ask them politely for this information:

- Excuse me, who is this?
- May (Can) I ask who is calling, please?

*Asking for Someone*

At other times, you'll need to speak to someone else. This is especially true when you telephone a business. Here are some examples:

- Can I have extension 321?
- Could I speak to...? (Can I—more informal/May I—more formal)

*Connecting Someone*

If you answer the phone, you might need to connect the caller to someone at your business. Here are some useful phrases:

- I'll put you through.
- Can you hold the line? /Can you hold on a moment?

*When Someone Is Not Available*

These phrases can be used to express that someone is not available to speak on the telephone.

- I'm afraid ... is not available at the moment.

- The line is busy ...
- Mr. Jackson isn't in .../Mr. Jackson is out at the moment...

*Taking a Message*

If someone isn't available, you might want to take a message to help the caller.

- Could (Can, May) I take a message?
- Could (Can, May) I tell him who is calling?

(adapted from website https://www.thoughtco.com/telephone-english-important-phrases-1210237)

Question 1: Is it true that using full name is more formal than using first name?

Question 2: Which language is common to answer the phone by stating the telephone number?

Question 3: Is it true that "May I speak to..." is more formal than "Could I speak to...?"

Question 4: If you need to connect the caller to someone at your business, what could you say?

## Project

Let us make a phone call to the university. Follow the steps.

Step 1: Visit website https://www.stmartin.edu/, and find relative phone numbers from contact information of Saint Martin's University.

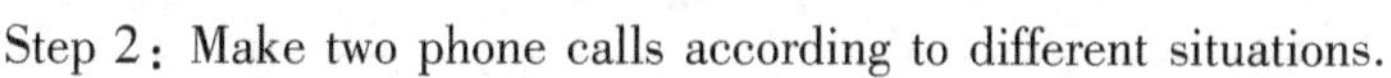

Step 2: Make two phone calls according to different situations.

Situation 1: You are a prospective student of Saint Martin's University. You failed to search some information of application so you plan to make a phone call to the international student center.

> Model dialogue
>
> A: Hello, this is student center. What can I do for you?
>
> B: Hello, this is ... (name) from China. I am planning to apply for your college recently, but I failed to search the deadline of application. Could you please tell me the way to ...?
>
> A: Sure ...

Dialogue 1:

(substitute: deadline, starting date, interview, requirement, enrollment, etc.)

________________________________________

________________________________________

________________________________________

Situation 2: You are current student of Saint Martin's University. You want to change the dormitory for personal issues so you made a phone call to the administrative office. But the staff there told you that you are expected to speak to staff in residential house and your line is transferred to the residential office.

Model dialogue

A: Good morning, this is Alex from administrative office. Who is calling?

B: Hi, I'm Jane from ... (department). I have some problems ... so I wonder if I could ...

A: Why don't you talk to the staff in the residential house?

B: I don't know how to find them.

A: Please hold the line. I will transfer you to... (place).

B: Thanks.

C: Hello, this is... (name).

B: Hello, this is .... (name). I have a problem ...

Dialogue 2:

(substitute: transfer, personal issue, living style, argument, conflict, interrupt, quiet environment, etc.)

______________________________________________

______________________________________________

______________________________________________

______________________________________________

# Unit 2  Traffic and Transport

## Learning Objectives

You are going to learn the following skills that are necessary for your living at abroad, not only for your short - time travelling but also for the long - time staying.

- You will learn about airline companies and how to book flight tickets online.
- You will learn to take the flight.
- You will learn to read the traffic information on the websites.
- You will learn to take different modes of transportation in the city.
- You will learn to rent a car at abroad.
- You will learn to make a personal itinerary.

# 1. Airline Company

**Pre - class Learning:** Watch the video and learn about airline companies and how to book flight tickets, then finish the following tasks.

**Topic:** Think about it and share your opinions on the online forum.

1. Have you ever booked flight tickets before? How do you book the ticket?
   (cues: phone, Internet, etc.)
2. Which airline companies do you know? What are the differences between airline companies?
   (cues: low - cost airline, spacious cabin, tasty food, cozy seat, five - star airline, etc.)

**Test:** Please watch the video online and answer the questions in the form.

Please answer the following questions according to what you have learned from the video.

1. Could you name some five - star companies?

2. What are features of low - cost airline companies?

3. Does low - cost airline mean that you have to pay for services?

4. What should you do if you want to select preferred seat during the booking period?

## Wordlist

Glossary

| return ticket | 往返票；回程票 | refund | 退款 |
|---|---|---|---|
| one - way ticket | 单程票 | cabin | 机舱 |
| stop over | 经停 | charge | 收费 |

续表

| depart | 出发 | available | 可用的 |
|---|---|---|---|
| premium | 优质的 | preferred | 优选的 |
| surcharge | 额外费用 | assigned | 已分配的 |
| flexible | 灵活的 | grand - total | 总价 |

## In - class Learning

### Skill Tips

*Knowledge about Airline Company*

• World's 5 star airlines from Skytrax

Skytrax is a United Kingdom - based consultancy which runs an airline and airport review and ranking site. Skytrax conducts research for commercial airlines, as well as taking surveys from international travelers to rate cabin staff, airports, airlines, airline lounges, in - flight entertainment, on - board catering, and several other elements of air travel.

• *Low - cost carrier*

A low - cost carrier or low - cost airline (occasionally referred to as no - frills, budget or discount carrier, and abbreviated as LCC) is an airline without most of the traditional services provided in the fare, resulting in lower fares and fewer comforts. To make up for revenue lost in decreased ticket prices, the airline may charge for extras such as food, priority boarding, seat allocating, and baggage.

### Reading Text

Rules of Cabin Baggage for Singapore Airline

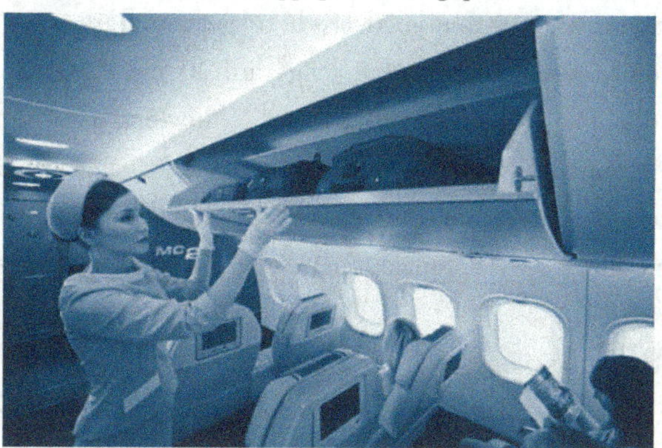

When you fly with us, you can carry up to two bags into the cabin with you depending on your class of travel.

For the safety, comfort and convenience of everyone on board, it's important for us to ensure that the overhead compartments are not excessively full and the cabin remains clutter – free.

If your cabin baggage exceeds these limits, it will be collected and stored in the aircraft cargo compartment. You may also have to pay for additional baggage charges if the combined weight or pieces of baggage exceeds your free allowance.

For the safety and comfort of our passengers, we have the right to determine that any baggage or item (s) in your baggage cannot be permitted in the cabin or on board our flight.

In addition to the limitations stated here, you must also be able to stow your baggage securely in the overhead compartment or under the seat in front of you.

Additional items allowed on board

You may carry ONE of these items with you on our flights, free of charge, in addition to your cabin baggage allowance (subject to country restrictions, where applicable):

- Ladies' handbag*
- Camera/Camera bag*
- Document bag*
- Overcoat
- Umbrella
- Laptop/Notebook in bag*
- Infant's amenities and food for consumption on board. The total weight of these items should not exceed 6 kg
- A walking stick, a pair of crutches and/or other prosthetic devices, if you are dependent on them
- A small amount of duty free goods (where permitted)

* The maximum dimensions for these bags are 40 cm × 30 cm × 10 cm each. If your item exceeds the total dimension of 80 $cm^3$ (the length, width and height combined), it will be counted as part of your standard cabin baggage allowance. You will then be required to check in either your cabin bag or the additional item.

(adapted from http://www.singaporeair.com/en_UK/au/travel-info/baggage/cabin-baggage/)

Question 1: How many bags can travelers carry into the cabin?

Question 2: What should be done if cabin baggage exceeds these limits?

Question 3: Is an umbrella allowed to be carried into the cabin?

Question 4: What is the restriction of infant's amenities?

## Project

Let us book a flight ticket online. Follow the steps.

Step 1: Visit website of Virgin Airline https://www.virginaustralia.com/au/en/.

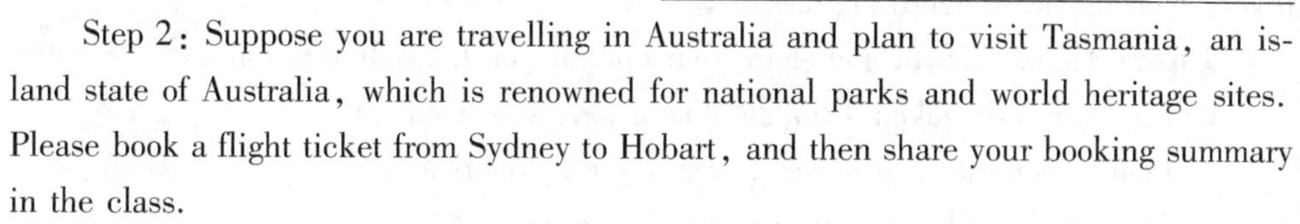

Step 2: Suppose you are travelling in Australia and plan to visit Tasmania, an island state of Australia, which is renowned for national parks and world heritage sites. Please book a flight ticket from Sydney to Hobart, and then share your booking summary in the class.

Step 3: Read an authentic e-ticket and find the relative information as requested.

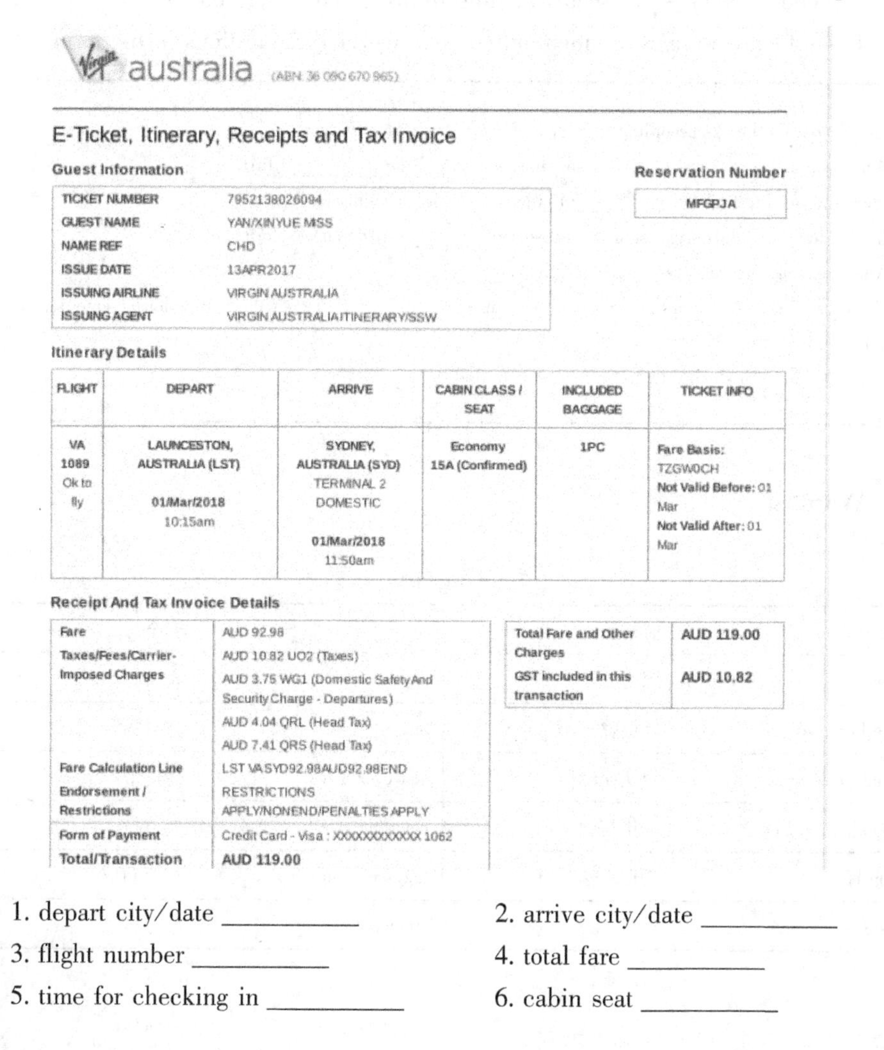

Virgin australia (ABN 36 090 670 965)

E-Ticket, Itinerary, Receipts and Tax Invoice

**Guest Information**

| | |
|---|---|
| TICKET NUMBER | 7952138026094 |
| GUEST NAME | YAN/XINYUE MISS |
| NAME REF | CHD |
| ISSUE DATE | 13APR2017 |
| ISSUING AIRLINE | VIRGIN AUSTRALIA |
| ISSUING AGENT | VIRGIN AUSTRALIA ITINERARY/SSW |

**Reservation Number**

MFGPJA

**Itinerary Details**

| FLIGHT | DEPART | ARRIVE | CABIN CLASS / SEAT | INCLUDED BAGGAGE | TICKET INFO |
|---|---|---|---|---|---|
| VA 1089 Ok to fly | LAUNCESTON, AUSTRALIA (LST) 01/Mar/2018 10:15am | SYDNEY, AUSTRALIA (SYD) TERMINAL 2 DOMESTIC 01/Mar/2018 11:50am | Economy 15A (Confirmed) | 1PC | Fare Basis: TZGWOCH Not Valid Before: 01 Mar Not Valid After: 01 Mar |

**Receipt And Tax Invoice Details**

| | |
|---|---|
| Fare | AUD 92.98 |
| Taxes/Fees/Carrier-Imposed Charges | AUD 10.82 UO2 (Taxes)<br>AUD 3.75 WG1 (Domestic Safety And Security Charge - Departures)<br>AUD 4.04 QRL (Head Tax)<br>AUD 7.41 QRS (Head Tax) |
| Fare Calculation Line | LST VA SYD92.98AUD92.98END |
| Endorsement / Restrictions | RESTRICTIONS APPLY/NONEND/PENALTIES APPLY |
| Form of Payment | Credit Card - Visa : XXXXXXXXXXXX1062 |
| Total/Transaction | AUD 119.00 |

| | |
|---|---|
| Total Fare and Other Charges | AUD 119.00 |
| GST included in this transaction | AUD 10.82 |

1. depart city/date __________
2. arrive city/date __________
3. flight number __________
4. total fare __________
5. time for checking in __________
6. cabin seat __________

## 2. Take the Flight

**Pre－class Learning:** Watch the video and learn the process of taking the flight, then finish the following tasks.

**Topic:** Think about it and share your opinions on the online forum.

1. Have you ever taken a flight? Where have you been?
   (cues: domestic, oversea, Europe, south America, etc.)
2. Can you describe the process of taking a flight?
   (cues: check－in, security, drop the bag, boarding, etc.)

**Test:** Please watch the video online and answer the questions in the form.

Please fill out the blanks according to what we have learned from the video.

1. When you arrive at the airport, you are supposed to find the ________at first.
2. Then you need to find the ________ in order to get your boarding pass.
3. If you have heavy luggage, you are supposed to ________ at the check－in counter.
4. After checking in, you need to go through the ________ .
5. When you arrive at the destination, you will go to the ________ to get the permission of entering into the country.
6. The last thing you should do in the airport is to find the ________ .

### Wordlist

Glossary

| terminal | 航站楼 | security | 安全 |
|---|---|---|---|
| domestic | 国内的 | custom | 海关 |
| boarding pass | 登机牌 | bin | 塑料箱 |
| metal detector | 金属探测器 | conveyor belt | 传送带 |
| check－in counter | 登机柜台 | boarding gate | 登机口 |
| drop bag | 托运行李 | luggage claim | 行李领取 |
| scale | 称重 | attendant | 服务员 |

## In – class Learning

### Skill Tips

*The process of taking a flight*

Step 1: find the international terminal

Step 2: get the boarding pass and drop bags

Step 3: go through the security check

Step 4: board on plane

Step 5: fill out your arrival record

Step 6: go through the custom desk

Step 7: claim your luggage

*Useful expressions at airport*

Check – in counter

- May I see your passport?
- Is there anyone else travelling with you?
- Are you checking in bags? /How many bags do you check – in?
- Please drop your baggage up here.
- Here is your boarding pass and luggage tag.
- Your luggage is overweight/oversized. You have to remove some belongings.

Security check

- Please lay your bags flat on your convey or belt.
- Please put your electronic devices in the bin.
- Please take off your jacket and belt.
- Please step back. Do you have anything in your pockets?

Airport announcement

- There has been a gate change.
- United Airline Flight 880 to Miami is now boarding.
- Please have your boarding pass and identification ready for boarding.

- We would like to invite our first and business – class passengers to board.
- This is the final boarding call for United Airlines Flight 880 to Miami.
- Passenger John Smith, please proceed to the United Airlines desk at Gate 12.

Custom desk

- What is your purpose of visiting…?
- How long will you stay here?
- Do you have your return ticket?
- Please place your finger on the scanner.

**Reading Text**

Airline Food: How to Order a Special Meal When Travelling Internationally

You may not be satisfied with the airline food that you are served when you are travelling. Airline food is not freshly prepared and it is usually not as nutritious as food that is offered in restaurants or prepared at home. While standard meals that are served by international airlines can reduce hunger, they may not be able to meet every passenger's dietary requirements.

You may have certain illnesses, health and weight – loss goals, or religious commitments that do not allow you to consume standard airline food. To meet the needs of their customers, most international airlines have a selection of special meals that are acceptable to people with dietary restrictions. Different international airlines offer different selections of meals, and you can find out about the special meals that are offered by your airline by visiting its website.

It is common practice for international air passengers to order special meals when they check in. Although airlines accept requests for special meals during check – in, they cannot guarantee that the meals will be available. They need more time to make preparations for special meals to be delivered to the right airplanes. The best thing to do is to call your airline and order your special meal a day or two before the date of your departure. Let the agent know your specific dietary requirements and he or she will make the necessary arrangements for you. When you are checking in at the airport you should ask the agent to check the computer to make sure that the airline has taken note of your request for a special meal. There should be a note on your boarding pass indicating that you have ordered a special meal.

In the event that there is a change of carrier, you should call your airline to make sure that your request for a special meal will be carried over to the other airplane. If a flight delay causes you to miss your connecting flight, the best you can do is to order your special meal when you are checking in for the next connecting flight.

(adapted from https://www.fitday.com/fitness – articles/nutrition/5 – celebs – who – have – joined – forces – with – fitness – brands – to – create – a – line – of – sneakers.html)

Question 1: Why do some passengers have special requirements for the food on the plane?

Question 2: Where do passengers find different special meals offered by different airlines?

Question 3: What is the best time to order the special food?

Question 4: What should the passenger do, if the carrier is changed?

## Project

Let us do the role play. Suppose you are taking the flight and please make dialogues in different situations. Follow the steps.

Step 1: Please review the dialogues from online classes which include situations of check – in desk, security check, on – board service, airport announcement, custom desk, luggage claim.

Step 2: Suppose you are an international traveler. Make dialogues according to different situations.

Situation 1: Suppose you are at the international terminal and try to find the check – in counter.

Model dialogue

A: Excuse me, Could you tell me where ... (place) is?

B: Sure, go down this way and you will see a MacDonald ... (place) is behind the MacDonald.

A: Thanks.

B: That's all right.

Dialogue 1:

(substitute: go straight down, opposite, on the corner of, go up/down with escalator, etc.)

______________________________________________

______________________________________________

______________________________________________

______________________________________________

Situation 2: Suppose you are on the plane and ask service from a flight attendant.

> Model dialogue
>
> A: Excuse me, can I have ... please?
>
> B: Sure, here you are.
>
> A: Thanks.

Dialogue 2:

(substitute: blanket, hot water, earplug, etc.)

______________________________________________

______________________________________________

______________________________________________

______________________________________________

Situation 3: Suppose you want to find your baggage claim.

> Model dialogue
>
> A: Excuse me, can you help me?
>
> B: Sure.
>
> A: Where can I get my luggage?
>
> B: Oh, the luggage claim is on the first floor. You could follow the signs for the luggage claim.

Dialogue 3:

(substitute: custom desk, luggage claim, sign, electronic screen, etc.)

______________________________________________

______________________________________________

______________________________________________

______________________________________________

# 3. City Transportation Site

**Pre - class Learning:** Watch the video and learn how to take city transportation, then finish the following tasks.

**Topic:** Think about it and share your opinions on the online forum.

1. Can you name some modes of city transportation? What are they?
   (cues: bus, ferry, light rail, etc. )
2. When you are in a strange city, how will you find the information of transportation?
   (cues: apps, Internet, ask a native, etc. )

**Test:** Please watch the video online and answer the questions in the form.

| Please answer the following questions according to what you have learned from the video. |
|---|
| 1. How many modes of city transportation have been mentioned in the video? What are they? |
| 2. How do we pay for the traffic fare in the modern society? |
| 3. What kind of websites are comparably reliable? |
| 4. Where can we find traffic information? |

**Wordlist**

Glossary

| | | | |
|---|---|---|---|
| underground/tube | 地铁 | monorail | 单轨列车 |
| light railway | 轻轨 | shuttle bus | 往返班车 |
| sightseeing bus | 观光车 | ferry | 渡轮 |
| smart card | 智能卡 | fare | 车票 |
| single ticket | 单程票 | benefit | 福利 |

## In - class Learning

### Skill Tips

*Key information on transport sites*

| Transport Website | | |
|---|---|---|
| Plan your trip<br>real time trip<br>planning | Route information<br>timetable or map | Transport apps |
| News<br>Transport<br>news and updates | Get your smart<br>card | Find services and<br>book your tickets online |

- What is the smart card?

Smart card is operated by a smart ticketing system used to pay for travel on public transport in city areas. Add value before you travel and tap on and off to pay your fare.

Smart cards are available over the counter from most retailers, including most convenience stores and news agents.

There are lots of benefits of using a smart card, including cheaper fares and daily and weekly fare caps. Concessions will be applied for specific groups. If you don't have a smart card, you can purchase single trip tickets on most services, however prices are more expensive than using a smart card.

### Reading Text

The London Underground (The Tube)

The main source of public transport in London revolves around the Underground (or the Tube as it is known to Londoners). This extensive network of 12 lines can get you to most places in the Centre of the city quickly. Delays on the Tube are not uncommon, so look out for service updates immediately beyond the ticket barriers at most stations or listen for announcements on the platforms. However, even with a delay here or there, the Tube is often the fastest way to cover a large amount of ground.

Trains and platforms are described as Eastbound, Westbound, Northbound or Southbound depending on the direction of the line and the station. The front of the train, and the platform indicator, will show the ultimate destination of the train which is usually (though not always) the last station on the line. If it still be confusing, but don't despair, help is at hand: Tube staff are knowledgeable about the system and can always be found at station ticket barriers and also on most platforms. It's also very helpful to pick up one of the free maps available at all train station ticket offices. Each line has its own unique color so it is easy to identify each line on maps and signs throughout the system. Similar maps in a variety of languages can also be found online.

It is always cheaper to use an Oyster Card than buy single tickets. Using an Oyster card, a single fare is £ 2.30 if you are travelling within the central Zone 1. So the most affordable way to ride the Tube all day to your heart's content is to buy an Oyster Card.

It's best to avoid the peak hours of travel on the Tube, both to save money and to avoid thinking you've just boarded the last train out of Calcutta as everyone squishes their way into the overcrowded car. And don't forget to heed the "Mind the Gap" announcements that will continuously remind you at many stops.

(adapted from https://www.tripadvisor.com/Travel-g186338-s303/London:United-Kingdom:Public.Transportation.html)

Question 1: How many lines of the underground revolving in London?

Question 2: Do maps at all train station ticket offices charge?

Question 3: What is the name of smart card in London?

Question 4: Why should you avoid peak hours?

**Project**

Let us read a transportation website and finish the task below.

Step 1: Enter website https://tfl.gov.uk/.

Step 2: Read the websites and answer the questions.

1. How many public transport could an oyster card be used in London?
2. If you are using TFL Rail services to travel, please find out single fare between Heathrow and Paddington by using single fare finder.

Step 3: Let us act out role – plays. Suppose you are planning to travel around London and have no idea of city transport. Ask a staff at information center about city transport.

Model dialogue

A: Excuse me, I am planning a day – trip in London. Could you tell me the easiest way to go around the city?

B: The easiest way to go around the city is …

A: How to pay the fare? /Where can I get the timetable?

B: …

Dialogue 1:

(substitute: traffic line, method of payment, modes of transportation, etc.)

________________________________________

________________________________________

________________________________________

________________________________________

## 4. Modes of City Transportation

**Pre – class Learning:** Watch the video and learn how to take city transportation, then finish the following tasks.

**Topic:** Think about it and share your opinions on the online forum.

1. What is your favorite mode of transportation to travel around the city?
   (cues: bus, ferry, train, tube, etc. )
2. Can you read the timetable and route of city transport? What information should be concerned?
   (cues: opening hour, fare, route, stop, etc. )

**Test:** Please watch the video online and answer the questions in the form.

| Train Transport Distance | Adult Opal card fare | Adult Opal single trip ticket fare |
|---|---|---|
| 0 – 10 km | $3. 46<br>( $2. 42 off – peak) | $4. 20 |
| 10 – 20 km | $4. 30<br>( $3. 01 off – peak) | $5. 20 |
| 20 – 35 km | $4. 94<br>( $3. 45 off – peak) | $6. 00 |
| 35 – 65 km | $6. 61<br>( $4. 62 off – peak) | $8. 00 |
| 65 + km | $8. 50<br>( $5. 95 off – peak) | $10. 20 |

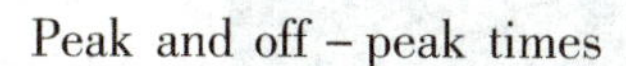

Peak and off – peak times

When using an Opal card on the train, you receive a 30 per cent fare discount when travelling on weekends. Public holidays and outside of the peak times below. Note: During the week. Morning peak travel times can vary for some intercity stations, depending on which station you tap on.

Please fill out the blanks according to information provided above.

1. If the distance is between 10 – 20 km, the adult Opal card fare is ______ at off – peak time.
2. If the distance is between 0 – 10 km, the adult Opal single trip ticket fare is ________.
3. If you purchase an Opal card, you will receive ________ discount when travelling on weekends, public holidays and out of peak times.

**Wordlist**

Glossary

| | | | |
|---|---|---|---|
| route | 线路 | receipt | 收据 |
| timetable | 时刻表 | interchange | 换乘 |
| valid | 有效 | line | 线路 |
| platform | 站台 | figure out | 弄清楚 |

## In – class Learning

### Skill Tips

*Useful information for city transportation*

● In some cities, transport fares between two stations may vary depending on the direction of travel, time of day (peak time/off – peak time) and day of the week (weekdays/weekends).

• In some cities, taxi fare may vary from color of the cars, time of day (peak time/off - peak time), and distance you go. You are not allowed to stop taxi everywhere. You could only wait for a taxi at taxi stand zone. There are several ways to take a taxi. Telephoning a taxi will cost you more. Therefore calling a taxi by apps may save you money.

• The service hour and route of public transport may vary a lot depending on day of the week, holidays and conditions. So please check it out online or through apps to find alerts for special routes.

*Useful expressions when asking for traffic information*

• Excuse me, could you please tell me which bus I should take to go to ...?

• Excuse me, I am transferring to Line 4, could you tell me which platform I should go?

• Hi, I am wondering where I can buy the single ticket for shuttle bus.

• I am going to ... Could you tell me how much of the ferry fare?

• How long does it take to go for a single trip?

## Reading Text

How to Ride a Bus

Get a bus pass or cash to pay the fare. You have to pay a fare if you want to ride a bus. Most people who use the bus frequently buy a pass and use it for efficiency and ease. You can usually purchase a bus pass at the city's public transportation website and/or office. If you aren't interested in getting a bus pass, you can also just pay in cash each time you ride the bus. Just make sure to bring exact change, as most city bus drivers aren't authorized to make change for you.

Some public transportation systems offer a discounted rate for seniors and/or people with disabilities. You can apply for this discounted rate at your city's public transportation website and/or office and then potentially receive a special bus pass that allows you to use the bus for a lower fare.

Arrive at the bus stop a few minutes prior to arrival. Most public transportation systems run smoothly so that they're reliable and predictable. Because of this, being late to the bus stop by just 1 – 2 minutes could mean missing your bus. To avoid this, make sure to get to the stop at least a few minutes before the bus is supposed to be arriving.

Look at the banner to make sure it's the right bus. Most public transportation buses have a digital banner on the front and/or side of the bus that displays the destination of the bus and/or the particular route name or number that the bus takes. As the bus approaches, read the banner to make sure that it's the right bus.

Wait for passengers to get off before you get on. After you've stepped onto the bus, you'll need to pay the required fare. If you have a bus pass, show it to the bus driver or scan it, if there's a place to do so. If you don't have a pass, simply put your cash through the slit in the fare box.

If you aren't sure what amount of cash to pay, check the fare box for a sign that displays the amount that's required.

(adapted from website https://www.wikihow.com/Ride-a-Public-Transportation-Bus)

Question 1: If you frequently use the bus, what is a good way to pay the fare?

Question 2: Where can you purchase the pass?

Question 3: Why should you bring the exact change if you don't want to buy a bus pass?

Question 4: How to make sure it's the right bus?

## Project

Let us read a website of city transport and then collect useful information as much as possible. Follow the steps.

Step 1: Visit website https://transportnsw.info/ and browse the page thoroughly.

Step 2: Click "travel information" and select "train" option. Then download the map of intercity train's network.

Step 3: Answer the questions below according to the intercity train map.

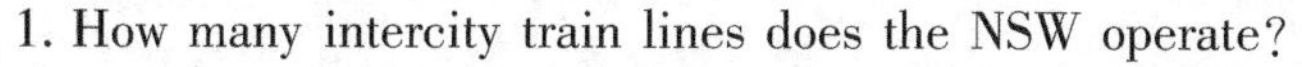

1. How many intercity train lines does the NSW operate?

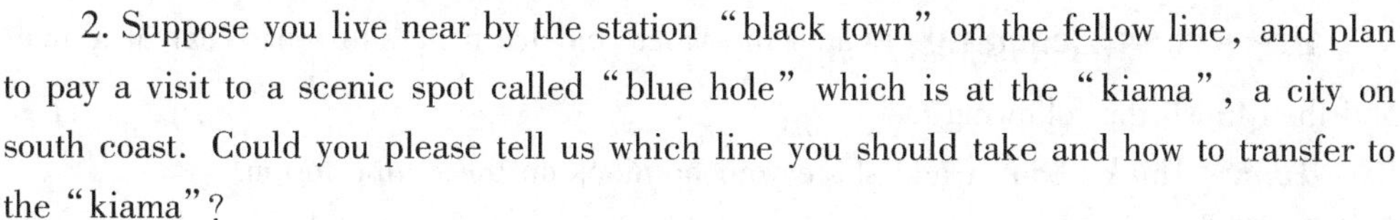

2. Suppose you live near by the station "black town" on the fellow line, and plan to pay a visit to a scenic spot called "blue hole" which is at the "kiama", a city on south coast. Could you please tell us which line you should take and how to transfer to the "kiama"?

3. Suppose you couldn't figure out the direction when transferring to the other line. Make a dialogue of asking a staff in the train station for the direction.

Model dialogue

A: Excuse me. May I ask you some questions?

B: Sure.

A: I am heading for ... but I can't figure out the direction. Could you please tell me which line I should transfer to?

B: Line ..., you may check it out on the electronic board.

A: Thanks.

Dialogue 1:

(substitute: place name, train station, direction, etc.)

# 5. Car Rental at Abroad

**Pre – class Learning:** Watch the video and learn how to rent a car at abroad and then finish the following tasks.

**Topic:** Think about it and share your opinions on the online forum.

1. Which car rental companies have you ever heard of?

   (cues: herz, European car, avis, etc. )

2. Could you say some tips for renting a car?

   (cues: driver license, car type, visual inspection, etc. )

**Test:** Please watch the video online and answer the questions in the form.

Please fill out the blanks according to what you have learned from the video.

1. If you are under the age of 25 years old, you will be charged ________.
2. If you return a car to a different location, you will be charged ________ .
3. When you pick a car at the counter, you had better provide two documents: ________ and ________.
4. How many things will be taken into account when choosing a car?

________________________

**Wordlist**

Glossary

| | | | |
|---|---|---|---|
| compact car | 紧凑型轿车 | automatic transmission | 自动挡 |
| intermediate car | 中型轿车 | suitcase | 行李箱 |
| full – size car | 大型车 | child seat | 儿童椅 |
| premium car | 尊贵型轿车 | vehicle | 机动车 |
| van | 面包车 | airbag | 安全气囊 |
| convertible | 敞篷车 | insurance | 保险 |
| manual | 手动挡 | unlimited kilometers | 无限公里数 |
| license | 驾照 | coverage | 保险范围 |
| sign | 签名 | plate | 牌照 |

## In – class Learning

### Skill Tips

*Knowledge about car rental policy*

• Most car rental companies maintain a 100% smoke – free fleet in the USA and Canada, and any type of smoking (pipe, cigarette, and cigar) is prohibited in all leased vehicles.

• If you want to make any modification of your car rental agreement, such as changing your return location, you have to contact the car rental company in advance. Most car rental companies have the branches all over the world. So keep the appropriate phone number of the targeted country for calling.

• Vehicles are rented on a daily (24 – hour) basis. There is a 29 – minute grace period for returns. After 30 minutes late, hourly car rate charges and taxes may apply. After 90 minutes late, full – day late charges and taxes may apply. After 7 hours late, if you didn't call to extend your rental, an additional $10/day late fee applies. There is no grace period for rental fees, surcharges and optional equipment or protections charges. Full – day late charges will apply for these items.

## Reading Text

How to Get a Discount Car Rental Rate

1. *Using Online Resources to Save Money*

• Use travel websites. Travel websites like Expedia, Hotwire, Travelocity, etc. offer a "one stop shop" for items like hotels and car rentals. These websites allow you to search for car rentals in specific locations and for a specific time frame, but unlike a car rental agency's website, you can compare the prices between multiple companies.

• Search for deals on consolidated car rental websites. In addition to travel websites that offer deals on multiple types of travel items (e. g. hotels, flights, etc.), there are also websites that specialize in car rental deals. Two well - known sites are CarRentals. com and AutoRentals. com.

• Look for deals on airline or hotel websites. Many major hotel chains and airlines partner with car rental agencies offer their customers special discounts. For airlines, you can often find information pertaining to car rental discounts right on their websites. For hotels, you can speak to someone at the concierge desk, or visit the car rental agency right inside the hotel.

2. *Getting Discounts Directly from the Rental Car Company*

• Agree to pay for your rental early. Some rental car companies will provide you with a discount if you pay for the entire rental up - front. This can be especially helpful when the car you're renting has unlimited mileage, so you know the price you're paying up - front will not change later.

• Join a rental car company's frequent renter program. Most car rental agencies have loyalty programs that give points to frequent renters. Signing up for such programs is usually free, and may even provide other advantages.

• Increase your rental time. Car rental agencies will charge a lower price per day the longer you rent a car. For example, booking a car for 1 week will be cheaper than if you book it for 6 days. If you're able to book a car for a longer period of time, you'll pay less per day.

(adapted from website https://www.wikihow.com/Get-a-Discount-Car-Rental-Rate)

Question 1: What is the advantage of renting a car through the travel websites?

Question 2: Can you name two well-known car rental websites?

Question 3: What advantage can you take of if you pay for your rental early?

Question 4: What other ways can you use to lower rental fee per day?

## Project

Let us book a car online. Follow the steps.

Step 1: Visit the website https://www.avis.com/en/home and browse the whole website thoroughly.

Step 2: Suppose you are travelling in the USA and plan to rent a car from New York airport and return the car to Washington airport. Please rent a car and then share your booking summary in the class.

Step 3: Let us simulate a dialogue at counter of Car Rental Company. Suppose you are going to pick up the leased car at the airport.

Model dialogue

A: Good afternoon. Can I help you?

B: Yes, I have a reservation for a car.

A: What is your last name on reservation?

B: It is...

A: Just one moment. I have a reservation for... picking up today and returning on the ...

B: Yes, that's right. I reserved a ...car.

A: Well, we do reserve a ... car for you. Would you like to purchase insurance for the car?

B: No, thanks.

A: Okay, then just sign here to decline the insurance. Be sure to return the car with a full gas tank or you'll be charged $3.00 per gallon.

B: Okay, I'll do that.

A: Here is your contract. Your car is in the parking lot space number W34.

B: Thanks. I appreciate it very much.

Dialogue 1:
(substitute: car type, date, fee, etc.)

________________________________________________

________________________________________________

________________________________________________

________________________________________________

Step 4: Read an authentic car rental agreement and find the relative information as requested.

1. Which car rental company does this agreement belong to?
2. What is the type of vehicle?
3. What is the rental period?
4. What extra fee does this agreement include?
5. How much deposit does the renter pay on initiation?

## 6. Plan a Route

**Pre – class Learning:** Watch the video and learn how to rent a car oversea, then finish the following tasks.

**Topic:** Think about it and share your opinions on the online forum.

1. Have you planned your trip before? How do you start your trip?
   (cues: travel agent, travel website, apps, etc.)
2. Do you have any skills to figure out the direction?
   (cues: policeman, security, map, etc.)

**Test:** Please watch the video online and answer the questions in the form.

| Please answer the following questions according to what you have learned from the video.<br>1. What is the trip planner used for?<br>2. In the example, label T usually stands for ________, label F stands for ________, label B stands for ________. |
|---|

**Wordlist**

Glossary

| itinerary | 行程 | trip planner | 旅行规划师 |
|---|---|---|---|
| apps | 应用程序 | light rail | 轻轨 |

**In – class Learning**

**Skill Tips**

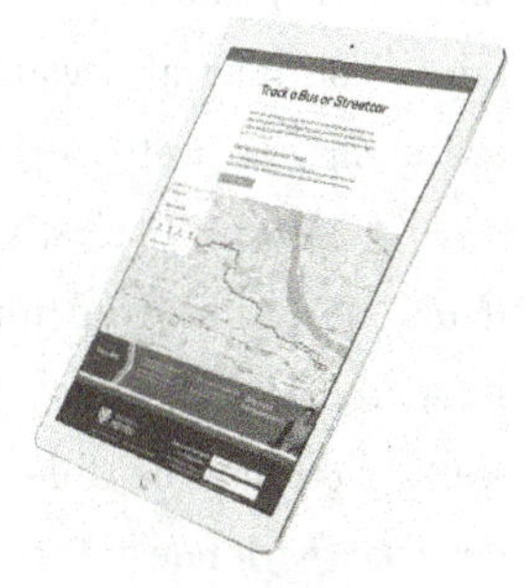

*How to Use Google Map*

Google Maps can be useful to navigate through a new location or place. You can also use it to find the best route or route alternatives, and plan your trip accordingly. You can get turn by turn directions, and different routes depending on your method of transportation. You will also be able to tell how long it will take to get to your destination. Here are some steps to make a route with google map:

Step 1: Identify your starting location and destination.

Step 2: Add more stops to rearrange your route.

Step 3: Select a transportation mode.

Step 4: View your routes.

Step 5: Select your routes.

Step 6: You may plan your own route by clicking on the icon of your desired stop.

**Reading Text**

How to Create a Travel Itinerary

1. *Planning and Mapping Your Itinerary*

• Collect the important information for your trip. Flight numbers, hotels, car rentals, and restaurant reservations are all key pieces of information to manage and maintain. You may also want to include directions to your hotel, the car rental company you are using, as well as directions to the airport for your return flight.

• Make a list. It's helpful to list all of the things you want to do on your trip. Even if it's more than you think you can manage, create a list of everything you'd like to do. Research local events, holidays, and observances of the places you're travelling too as well. You may be able to witness or experience a cultural event that other travelers don't get to experience.

• Map your stops. Match your stops to specific locations on a map and note their locations. Try and map them sequentially to efficiently use your travel time. You'll most likely be travelling from adjacent cities as you travel. For each activity, estimate the length of time it will take to get to there, and how long you will be there.

• Create a budget. Do you want a trip with days spent at four star restaurants and nights spent in five star hotels? Or are you more interested in finding local favorites and rustic B&BS? It ultimately comes down to what you can afford.

- Stay flexible. Don't hesitate to give yourself a free day or two. You can use this free day to explore, or take some time off to rest.

2. *Organizing Your Itinerary*

- Record your information. Record your check in times, confirmation numbers, hotel names, and any other information you might need on hand. Don't worry about organizing this information yet.

- Organize your travel information. Try and condense your travel information into a single document for easy access while travelling. Keep a printed copy or type the details of your itinerary into a word processing document.

- Keep a hard-copy. Your travel itinerary can be placed into a 3-ring binder. As convenient as an app can be, batteries can die. It never hurts to keep a physical backup handy. Use page dividers to separate documents in your trip binder into categories (rental car, tours, hotel reservations, etc.).

(adapted from https://www.wikihow.com/Create-a-Travel-Itinerary)

Question 1: How much information do you need to collect before you start your trip?

Question 2: What is the advantage of researching local events, holidays, the places you're travelling?

Question 3: What is a good idea to organize your travel information?

Question 4: Why do you need to have a physical backup handy?

## Project

Let us plan a route together by using trip planner. Follow the steps.

Step 1: Many oversea cities have trip planners in their transportation websites. Actually it is an effective way to plan the route before you arrive in the destination. Now please enter website https://transportnsw.info/.

Step 2: Suppose you are flying to Sydney. Now you have to make a route from the airport to the hotel and then go to the Manly beach, a famous scenic spot in Sydney. Please use the trip planner and tell us how to make the route.

| Model structure |
|---|
| I have found several ways to go to the hotel. First I should take..., then ... |
| From the hotel, I can take... to go to the Manly beach. |

（cue：Your hotel is “Radisson hotel and suites” which is located in Liverpool Street.）

____________________________________________________________

____________________________________________________________

____________________________________________________________

____________________________________________________________

# Unit 3 Tourism

Learning Objectives

You are going to learn the following skills that are necessary for your travelling abroad.

➢ You will learn to read tourism websites.

➢ You will learn to start a self-guided tour.

➢ You will learn to travel with agency.

➢ You will learn to book hotel rooms on official sites.

➢ You will learn to communicate with the hotel staff.

➢ You will learn the knowledge of the Visa.

# 1. Tourism Website

**Pre – class Learning:** Watch the video and learn to read tourism information on the websites, then finish the following tasks.

**Topic:** Think about it and share your opinions on the online forum.

1. Do you like travelling? Which place is your dream destination?
   (cues: domestic city, oversea city, etc.)
2. Have you ever visit tourism website before? Which content does it contain?
   (cues: map, timetable, location, fare, etc.)

**Test:** Please watch the video online and fill out the form below.

Here is detailed information of Singapore Flyer. Please fill out the blanks below.

Flight Schedule

Daily flights: 8:30 am – 10:30 pm

The first flight is at 8:30 am and the last flight is at 10:15 pm. The entire experience includes the Journey of Dreams and one rotation (30 minutes) on Singapore Flyer.

Would you like to upgrade to a Premium Champagne Flight or a Private Capsule?

Ticketing Counter

Ticketing Counter Operating Hours: 8:00am – 10:00pm

Ticket counter is located at the entrance of the 1st floor.

|  |  |
| --- | --- |
| Adult<br>(13 years or older) | $33 |
| Child<br>(3-12 years old) | $21 |
| Senior<br>60 years old and above<br>(Only Singapore Citizens and Permanent Residents are eligible to purchase.) | $24 |

续表

. For senior tickets, guests will be required to present their NRIC for age verification.

. Children below the age of 3 are allowed to ride for free.

1. The first flight of the flyer is ________, and the last flight is ________.

2. One rotation of the flyer is ________.

3. The ticket counter is located at ________.

4. Ticket for 5 year – old child is ________.

## Wordlist

Glossary

| | | | |
|---|---|---|---|
| brochure | 宣传册 | schedule | 时间表 |
| promotion | 促销 | voucher | 代金券 |
| tourist attraction | 观光胜地 | demonstration | 展示 |
| camping site | 露营地 | package | 套餐 |
| retreat | 疗养所 | resort | 度假村 |
| self – contained | 设施齐全的 | cabin | 小木屋 |

## In – class Learning

### Skill Tips

*Cultural information of tourism*

*Grand Tour*

Modern tourism can be traced to what was known as the Grand Tour, which was a traditional trip around Europe (especially Germany and Italy), undertaken by mainly upper – class European young men of means, mainly from Western and Northern European countries. In 1624, young Prince of Poland, the eldest son embarked for a journey across Europe, as was in custom among Polish nobility. He travelled through territories of today's Germany, Belgium, Netherlands, France, Switzerland to Italy, Austria, and the Czech Republic.

*Modern Day Tourism*

Many leisure – oriented tourists travel to seaside resorts on their nearest coast or further afield. Coastal areas in the tropics are popular in both summer and winter.

The World Tourism Organization reports the following ten destinations as the most visited in terms of the number of international travelers in 2017.

(https://en.wikipedia.org/wiki/Tourism)

| Rank | Country | UNWTO Region | International tourist arrivals (2017) |
|---|---|---|---|
| 1 | France | Europe | 86.9 million |
| 2 | Spain | Europe | 81.8 million |
| 3 | United States | North America | 75.9 million |
| 4 | China | Asia | 60.7 million |
| 5 | Italy | Europe | 58.3 million |
| 6 | Mexico | North America | 39.3 million |
| 7 | United Kingdom | Europe | 37.7 million |
| 8 | Turkey | Europe | 37.6 million |
| 9 | Germany | Europe | 37.5 million |
| 10 | Thailand | Asia | 35.4 million |

## Reading Text

London Eye, UK

The London Eye has now become one of the iconic sights of London. Opened in March 2000, the wheel is a metaphor for the turning of the century.

The London Eye is 135 m/443 ft high and weighs 2,100 tons.

There are 32 capsules attached to the wheel which travels gently at a speed of 26 cm per second. Each rotation takes 30 minutes in which time you can marvel at the views that span up to 40 km in all directions (depending on the weather).

This is the UK's most popular paid for visitor attraction, visited by over 3.5 million people a year.

There are also lots of special packages available.

The London Eye is within walking distance from several underground stations including Waterloo, Embankment, Charring Cross and Westminster. Waterloo is the closest tube station.

*Opening Times*

October to May—10:00 am - 8:00 pm daily

June—10:00 am - 9:00 pm daily

July—10:00 am - 9:30 pm daily

September—10:00 am - 9:00 pm daily

Not open on Christmas Day or during maintenance period from 11 to 20 January 2008.

*Ticket Prices*

Adult

- January to March 2008 £ 15.00
- April to December 2008 £ 15.50

Child (5 – 15 years old)

- January to March 2008 £ 7.50
- April to December 2008 £ 7.75

Child under 5 years old—free

Senior (60 plus) —£ 12.00

Disabled—£ 12.00

*Location Map*

Find out how to get to London Eye with directions and maps from Google.

The London Eye

Riverside Building

County Hall

Westminster Bridge Road

London

UK

(adapted from http://www.tourist – information – uk.com/london – eye.htm)

Question 1: What does London Eye stand for?

Question 2: How long does each rotation take?

Question 3: Which tube station is the closest to London Eye?

Question 4: What is the opening time of London Eye, if you go there in the summer holiday?

## Project

Let us visit tourism sites and search information together. Follow the steps.

Step 1: Enter the website http://www.tourist – information – uk.com/ and browse the whole page.

Step 2: Find UK tourist attractions column and pick one place that you are interested in except London Eye. Make a poster to introduce your scenic spot.

Directions: Each tourist attraction has its specialty. For example, you should pay more attention to the opening time and themes of museums and for most theme parks you are supposed to get more information about timetable of each activity and demonstration. Please collect as much information as possible for your poster.

______________________________

______________________________

______________________________

______________________________

Step 3: Make a dialogue of tourist enquiry according to your poster.

Model dialogue

A: Hi, may I ask some questions about London Eye tour?

B: Sure, go ahead.

A: What is London Eye famous for?

B: Well, it is one of the iconic sights in London which is a metaphor for the turning of century. It has 32 capsules where you can marvel at the views that span up to 40 km in all directions.

A: What is the opening hour?

B: Well, it depends on which month you arrive ...

A: How much is the ticket fare?

B: It varies from seasons and ages...

A: Thanks for your advice.

Dialogue 1:

______________________________

______________________________

______________________________

______________________________

## 2. Self – guided Tour

**Pre – class Learning:** Watch the video and learn how to start self – guided tour, then finish the following tasks.

**Topic:** Think about it and share your opinions on the online forum.

1. How do you prepare a self – guided tour?
   (cues: document, record, ticket, booking information, etc.)
2. Do you have any techniques of planning a self – guided tour? Share with others.
   (cues: tourism website, itinerary, reservation, map, etc.)

**Test:** Please watch the video online and fill out the form below.

Please answer the following questions according to what you have learned from the video.

1. In the zoo case, we learned that the roar and snore itinerary start from ________, and end at ________.
2. In the zoo case, we learned that the yellow chart means ________, the green chart means ________.
3. In the zoo case, we learned that fee for adult during off – peak time is ______ .

### Wordlist

Glossary

| | | | |
|---|---|---|---|
| self – guided tour | 自助游 | audio guide | 语音向导 |
| escort | 陪同 | virtual guide | 虚拟向导 |
| navigate | 导航 | pamphlet/booklet | 小册子 |

## In – class Learning

### Skill Tips

*Knowledge about self – guided tour*

A self – guided tour is a self – governing tour where one navigates a route oneself as opposed to an escorted tour where a tour guide directs the route, times, information, and places toured. Many tourist attractions provide suggestions, maps, instructions, directions, and items to see or do during self – guided tours.

As with escorted tours, self – guided tours may be conducted on foot or by vehicle. Audio tours are frequently presented in a self – guided format using booklets, smart phones or stand alone handheld devices, as are virtual tours.

*Where to get visitor information*

- bookstore
- pamphlet at airport or hotel
- travel website
- visitor information

*Aids for self – guided tour*

- smartphone tour guide
- handheld audio guide device
- day tour guide

## Reading Text

### London Walking Tours

Whether you're in town for a weekend in London or sightseeing for the day, our London tours cover popular tourist destinations as well as off the beaten path parts of town. We offer both guided tours and self – guided tours that take you through the heart of the city and Westminster and help you decide what to do in London and what to see.

Check out our tour calendar below or go straight to our booking page.

We have approximately 3,000 reviews with a rating of 5 out of 5 stars. Read the reviews for yourself.

And be sure to check out our guide to London tourist discount passes for more money saving ideas for your visit.

Regularly Scheduled Walking Tours of London

- Our Westminster Tour (Royal London Tour) takes in Buckingham Palace and the Changing of the Guard.
- City of London Walking Tour, which focuses on the old Roman settlement, St. Paul's Cathedral and the Tower of London.
- If you are short on time, then consider the ultimate of London walking tours, our London – All – in – One Tour, a six – hour adventure that combines both tours plus a bit more.
- Never got your letter from Hogwarts but still want to be a wizard? Come along on our Harry Potter Walking Tour to add some magic to your London trip!
- Fancy yourself a culture – vulture? Then check out the Royal Tour of Kensington to enjoy one of the best known (and best looking!) parts of London.
- Explore the museums with a local guide who can show you the highlights, from the British Museum and the National Gallery.
- And for the braver souls, our nighttime Jack the Ripper and London Ghost tours

are available, if you dare.

• For a taste of alternative side of the city, check out London Graffiti and Street Art Tour, which visits East London and covers the art, history, and culture of this exciting area.

(adapted from website https://freetoursbyfoot.com/london-tours/#walk)

Question 1: If the tourist is interested in Changing of the Guard, which tour will you recommend?

Question 2: If the tourist is a fan of Harry Potter, which tour will you recommend?

Question 3: If the tourist is short on time, which tour will you recommend?

Question 4: If the tourist is an artist, which tour will he or she probably go for?

## Project

Let us make a plan of self-guided tour. Follow the steps.

Step 1: Visit https://freetoursbyfoot.com/ which is a website for self-guided tour. Pick a city you want to go.

Step 2: Find a self-guided tour in your targeted city and collect enough information about the tour.

Step 3: Present your own self-guided tour as a group. We will see which group's itinerary will earn the most attention in the class.

Directions: You'd better answer the following questions before starting your presentation.

- What can we experience during the tour? What is the specialty of the tour?
- How long does it take?
- Any cost included?
- What is the route?
- What are the reviews from former tourists?

______________________________________________

______________________________________________

______________________________________________

______________________________________________

## 3. Guided Tour

**Pre - class Learning:** Watch the video and learn how to book guided tours, then finish the following tasks.

**Topic:** Think about it and share your opinions on the online forum.

1. What is the difference between self - guided tour and guided tour?
   (cues: planned route, travel specialist, save time, etc.)
2. Have you ever joined a guided tour? What do you think of guided tour?
   (cues: route, guide, schedule, group size, etc.)

**Test:** Please watch the video online and fill out the form below.

The following is an adverts of day tours. Please answer the questions according to what you have learned from the video.

Award Winning Day Tours

*The Blue Mountains Specialists*

We have 20 years' experience in taking small group tours to the Blue Mountains from Sydney and offer exceptional value, deluxe coaches and professional Australian Guides.

You will see all the main sights of Katoomba, the Three Sisters, and the Grand Canyon, take the exciting rides at Scenic World and can visit Featherdale Wildlife Park.

The tour operates EVERY DAY and we have free Sydney Hotel pickup.

Deluxe Mini Coaches Air - conditioned comfort Expert Drivers Guides Personalized Small Groups (Max 21) Free Hotel Pickup, City or North Small Groups. Only for Blue mountains and Hunter Valley tours (all other tours use a large luxury coach).

1. What is the maximum of the group size?

2. What is the nationality of the guide?

3. Do they offer free Sydney hotel pickup?

4. What is this tour's inclusions and highlights?

**Wordlist**

Glossary

| day tour | 一日游 | hiking tour | 徒步之旅 |
| --- | --- | --- | --- |
| highlight | 特色 | gourmet tour | 美食之旅 |
| cruise tour | 邮轮旅行 | wideness adventure | 野外探险 |
| wildlife interaction | 野生动物互动 | coach | 客车 |
| bushwalking | 丛林漫步 | guide | 导游 |

## In – class Learning

### Skill Tips

*The pros and cons of guided tour*

*Pros*

• Tour guides can offer a safer experience, especially if you're in a city or country known for not being the safest spot. Even if you're in a safe place (like Singapore), you may want to use a guide to help you navigate. In some countries, almost no locals speak English (this makes ordering food and asking for directions difficult) and signs will often not be in English.

• You get your own translator who can help you communicate both in terms of language and cultural practices. With their assistance, you'll be able to avoid getting yourself into sticky situations.

• Some activities, like river rafting and adventure sports, generally are not available without a guide.

• You may get discounts or special entry available only to tour groups. Some museums open early to let tour groups get a head start, then they let smaller or individual travelers filter through afterwards.

• You have a certain level of comfort with a guided tour. This applies both to accommodations and how you feel. If you don't have a lot of time to see the sights, using a tour guide will help you get the most out of your trip.

*Cons*

- A guided tour isn't the best deal for your money when a guidebook (or your own research) will work just fine.
- With a guided tour, you likely won't have total control over what and when you see.
- The cost of guided tours can eat into a tight travel budget. Tours are pretty expensive, even audio guides sometimes cost much.
- If your destination is pretty safe and you know the language, can get by without knowing the language, or you know someone who speaks the language, then you probably don't need a tour guide to help you get around.

**Reading Text**

Christchurch Guided Tour & Whale Watch Cruise

This full day tour includes a scenic tour from Christchurch through the rolling hill country of North Canterbury to Kaikoura; one of the few places in the world that can boast of such nature wonders as those offered by land and sea!

Once in Kaikoura you will have some free time to explore and enjoy lunch (at your own expense) before boarding a modern catamaran for an exciting whale watch tour!

Off the coast of the Kaikoura Village is a marine environment so rich in nutrients that it attracts some of the most magnificent creatures with which we share our planet. Among them the giant Sperm Whale which can grow up to 20 metres in length and has the largest brain of any animal alive.

Not only can you be introduced to the magnificent Sperm Whale, but also to migratory Humpback Whales (June & July), Orca (summer months), New Zealand's own tiny Hectors dolphin, the high spirited displays of the Dusky dolphins, New Zealand Fur seals and the Royal Albatross. After your encounter with the giants of the sea and marine life, return to Kaikoura.

On the conclusion of your tour, you will be returned to your accommodation in Christchurch.

Tour Info

Tour type: guided nature tours & walks

From: Christchurch to Christchurch

Price: from (NZD) $329 per person

Duration: 1 day

Tour code: HFKWW

Inclusions

√ Informative and entertaining commentary from our local kiwi guides

√ Pick up & drop off to centrally located accommodations

√ Scenic tour from Christchurch over the Canterbury plains to Kaikoura

√ Free time to explore Kaikoura

√ Whale watch cruise with whale watch Kaikoura

(adapted from website https://www.relaxingjourneys.co.nz/sightseeing_tours/hf/hfkww.php)

Question 1: What is the highlight of this tour?

Question 2: Does this tour include lunch?

Question 3: What is the highlight of Kaikoura Village?

Question 4: How long does this tour last?

**Project**

Let us book a whale watch tour together. Follow the steps.

Step 1: Visit website https://www.relaxingjourneys.co.nz/sightseeing_tours/hf/hfkww.php and find more information about the whale watch tour, for example single price, reviews, operating hour, etc.

Step 2: Make a role play of Q&A based on your collected information.

> Directions: Collect more details about the tour and make a dialogue between tourists and staff in the travel agency. Try to include as much details as possible.

Dialogue 1:

(cues: departure point/time; return details; anything related to the tour)

________________________________________________

________________________________________________

________________________________________________

________________________________________________

## 4. Book Hotel Room

**Pre – class Learning**: Watch the video and learn how to book room online, then finish the following tasks.

**Topic**: Think about it and share your opinions on the online forum.

1. Have you ever booked a hotel room before? How did you book the room? (cues: at counter, phone, online, etc.)
2. Which things will you take into consideration when booking a hotel room? (cues: rate, environment, security, facility, etc.)

**Test**: Please watch the video online and fill out the form below.

| Please answer the following questions according to what you have learned from the video. |
|---|
| 1. Can you name a few oversea hotel booking platforms? |
| 2. What is the advantage of booking a room on official site? |
| 3. If you need two beds in one room, which room type will you book? |
| 4. Why does the same room type have different room rate? |

### Wordlist

Glossary

| | | | |
|---|---|---|---|
| executive room | 行政房 | ocean view | 海景 |
| city view | 城市景观 | garden view | 花园景 |
| refundable | 可退款的 | include | 包含 |
| exclude | 不包含 | guest room | 客房 |
| king bed | 大床房 | double beds | 双床房 |

## In – class Learning

### Skill Tips

*Background information about hotel loyalty program*

A hotel loyalty program will generally have multiple levels. Newly joined members are offered some privileges, such as free Internet to encourage them to join the scheme. This ensures that the guest has an incentive to use their loyalty card, even if they do not anticipate reaching the next rewards level. In addition, joining the scheme and staying nights in a hotel will typically accrue points, which are similar to frequent flyer miles, and can be redeemed for free nights in hotels (the number of points required to stay a night may vary based on the normal cost of the hotel, and on the day of the week or season) and other benefits, such as a welcome gift, free parking, discount pricing, greater points earning and buying power, and/or no blackout dates.

### Reading Text

How Can You Get a Room Upgrade at a Hotel?

If you want a room upgrade—a better quality room for the price of a standard room—you have to ask. Although there are no guarantees, knowing how and when to ask just may land you that coveted room upgrade. Here are some techniques that may just land you that coveted upgrade.

When you book a stay during the hotel's off – season or a slow time of the week, your chances are better. And if you've had the opportunity to join the hotel's frequent visitor program, your request will have more clout.

*No Upgrade Yet? Ask Again. And Again.*

If the reservation desk can't upgrade you immediately, ask again a few days before your stay. Still no luck? Ask again when you check into the hotel. If they haven't booked a higher – price room by the time you arrive, the hotel manager may be willing to grant your request.

*Make a Connection*

It helps if you mention you're celebrating a special occasion like a birthday or an anniversary. But I don't recommend fibbing. It would be better to honestly tell the person you're dealing with your real story, such as "My wife has been working so hard with the kids, I'd love her to be able to enjoy her much – needed vacation with an upgraded room."

Connecting with hotel staff members you're talking to in a sincere, friendly way always makes a big impact.

*A Few More Upgrade Strategies*

- Frequent flier miles can be turned in for upgrades, but the exchange is only a good idea if you don't think you'll need the points for building credit for a free flight.
- If a hotel has seriously disappointed you with a significant service failure, such as not cleaning your room or mishandling your baggage, you can always suggest they can make it up to you with a room upgrade.
- And finally, if you're not already a member of the resort's loyalty program, join it so you will have a better chance for an upgrade the next time you stay.

(adapted from website https://www.tripsavvy.com/get – a – room – upgrade – 3880438)

Question 1: Is it true that you may have more chance to upgrade your room when it is hotel's off – season or a slow time of the week?

Question 2: In which circumstance will the hotel manager be willing to grant your request?

Question 3: What benefit will you have if you join the resort's loyalty program?

Question 4: If you unfortunately met a significant service failure, what could you suggest to make up?

**Project**

Let us make a reservation of the hotel room. Follow the steps.

Step 1: Suppose you are travelling to Bali Indonesia.

Please visit website http://hiltonhonors3.hilton.com/en/index.html.

Step 2: Enter "Bali Indonesia" with your expected date and then select "Hilton Bali Resort".

Step 3: Find your ideal room and explain the reason why you choose it.

Room Details: KING DELUXE OCEAN VIEW

1 of 4

48 sq. m., ocean view, balcony, marble bathroom

Admire the stunning views of the Indian Ocean from your balcony, this stylish 48 sq. m./516 sq ft. room is located on the North and South Wing. All rooms feature a comfortable seating corner for reading or relaxing and an elegant marble bathroom with modern amenities, separate shower and deep soaking tub.

Amenities include a 40-inch LCD TV with international channels, WiFi (fees apply), complimentary mineral water, in-room tea and coffee making facilities and waffle robes. This room has one king bed.

Sample:

I will choose king deluxe ocean view with rate of 2, 727, 685IDR. The reason why I choose this room type is that it has spacious interior space and comfortable bathroom with modern amenities, separate shower and deep soaking tub. From this room, I may admire the stunning views of the Indian ocean. What is more, it has free standard Wi – Fi in – room and in the lobby and it has free cancellation up to 21days before arrival.

________________________________________

________________________________________

________________________________________

________________________________________

## 5. Hotel Service

**Pre - class Learning**: Watch the video and learn how to communicate with hotel staff, then finish the following tasks.

**Topic**: Think about it and share your opinions on the online forum.

1. Can you explain how to check - in, and check out at hotel?
   (cues: passport, deposit, room key, etc. )
2. In which circumstances will you need to communicate with hotel staff?
   (cues: room service, club activities, tourist information, etc. )

**Test**: Please watch the video online and fill out the form below.

| Please answer the questions according to what you have learned from the video. |
|---|
| 1. What is an easy way to contact with an oversea hotel before arrival? |
| 2. Why did the guest ask for airport transfer in the video? |
| 3. Does the hotel in the video offer airport transfer? How much is it per person? |
| 4. What is the question of the guest who is chatting online with the hotel service? |

**Wordlist**

Glossary

| | | | |
|---|---|---|---|
| airport transfer | 机场接送 | in - room dinner | 房内就餐 |
| front desk | 前台 | custom desk | 海关柜台 |
| signage | 引导标识 | room preference | 房型偏好 |
| allocation | 配置，定位 | No smoking area | 无烟区 |
| swipe | 刷卡 | pre - authorization | 预授权 |

### In - class Learning

**Skill Tips**

*International hotel rules*

- Tariff

Room rate on the hotel site is not included tariff. The tariff is for the room only and is exclusive of any government taxes applicable. Meals and other services are available at extra cost.

- Arrival

Most western hotels' sites show check – in time is 2 pm, but if there is room vacancy at the time you arrive, you could still check – in. However, if you arrive at very early time like midnight you have to pay one day more.

- Departure

Most western hotels' sites show check out time is usually around 10 am. If you wish to retain your room beyond this time, the extension will be given depending on the availability. If the room is available, the normal tariff will be charged. On failure of the guest to vacate the room on expiry period, the management shall have the right to remove the guest and his/her belongings from the room occupied by the guest.

- Luggage Storage

Subject to availability of the storage space, the guest can store luggage in the luggage room, at the guest's sole risk as to loss or damage from any cause. Luggage may not be stored for a period of over 30 days.

- Guest's Belongings

Guests are particularly requested to lock the door of their rooms when going out or going to bed. For the convenience of the guest, electronic safety lockers are provided in the room to store any valuables.

- Pets

Check the pet policy when booking the hotel because not all hotels allow pets stay.

- Damage to Property

The guest will be held responsible for any loss or damage to the hotel property caused by themselves, their guests or any person for whom they are responsible.

## Reading Text

### Questions You Must Ask When Checking Into Your Hotel

You've researched your hotel, checked all the review sites, and even booked the room online. But there are a few questions that you can only ask in person, while you're checking in, that can make your trip much better. Here are four must - asks that can improve your stay—and help you avoid surprises when you check out.

*Is there a resort fee, and what does it include?*

Often, published rates don't include extras like taxes or resort fees, the often unavoidable extra charges that properties say cover services like Wi - Fi, parking, or the use of the fitness center. "Asking this question up front lets guests know what their final charges will be so that there aren't any surprises," says Michelle, front office assistant manager at B Resort & Spa in Orlando.

*Am I entitled to any exclusive amenities?*

Some hotels offer guests extra perks, especially if they booked their stay through a travel specialist that works closely with a particular hotel. "Our clients often receive hundreds of dollars in perks, credits, upgrades, and exclusive experiences," says Hughs Wood, a travel advisor.

*Are there any special hotel offerings that are not widely advertised?*

Even if you don't book with a travel specialist, the hotel might offer programs or services that aren't publicized. "I've found that some of my favorite hotel experiences are ones the hotel doesn't advertise," Hughs Wood says. "The Four Seasons Hotel George V in Paris has avid runners on its staff who came up with the idea of taking clients out for a casual, energetic morning run once a week through Paris at no charge. You wouldn't know about it unless you asked." Other hotels have running programs, too, including Westin, which even has a global running concierge.

*How is the traffic here?*

"Whether you're driving a rental car, taking a taxi, or riding public transportation, it's a really good idea to ask about the traffic," says Elizabeth Moriarty, vice president for product development with Delta Vacations. "'When is it heaviest?' or 'What's the fastest way to get where I'm going?' are questions that will help a traveler with planning out their days. Getting it out of the way at check in is the best idea."

(adapted from website https://www.cntraveler.com/stories/2015-06-19/seven-questions-you-must-ask-when-checking-in-to-your-hotel)

Question 1: From the text, which extras would not be included in the published rates?

Question 2: From the text, how can guests get extra perks?

Question 3: Who came up with the idea of taking clients out for a casual, energetic morning run?

Question 4: Why does the guest ask about the traffic?

## Project

Let us do the role play. Suppose you are staying at a resort and please make dialogues in different situations.

Situation 1: Suppose you are talking with the front desk.

Model dialogue

A: Good afternoon, madam, Welcome to Hilton resorts. What can I do for you?

B: Yes, I'd like to check-in please.

A: Certainly, madam. May I have your passport please?

B: Here you are.

A: Thank you for waiting Ms. Li. Your reservation is for a guest room with ocean view for two nights. The room rate is $ 230 per night. Is that all right?

B: Yes, that is right.

A: Well, do you want to pay by credit card or by cash?

B: By credit card.

A: Well, Ms. Li, please show me your credit card, I'll swipe $ 500 of pre-authorization as your deposit. Do you have a password of your card?

B: Yes.

A: Please input the password.

A: The breakfast time is from 7:00 am to 10:00 am at the main hall. Please show your room number before the meal.

B: OK, I get it.

A: Your room number is 1018. Here is your key card. The bellman will take your luggage and show you the way.

B: Thanks a lot.

Dialogue 1:

(substitute: room update, room service, facilities, etc.)

Situation 2: Suppose you are calling for room service.

Model dialogue

A: Good evening, this is Hilton resort service center. May I help you?

B: Yes, I'd like to have someone to tidy up the bathroom. We've just showered, and it's quite a mess here. Please bring me more clean towels.

A: Yes, madam. The housekeeper will be there soon.

B: Thank you very much.

A: You are welcome.

Dialogue 2:

(substitute: in – room dinner, find hair dryer, housekeeping, etc.)

Situation 3: Suppose you are enquiring for entertainment activities.

Model dialogue

A: Hello, what can I do for you?

B: Well, I'd like to know how I can rent a bike.

A: It is free to hotel guest for one hour. If you delay to return the bike after one hour you have to pay rental fee of 10 dollars per hour.

B: OK, do you have recommended routes to go?

A: Yes, here is a map for you. We highly recommend you to ride around lake nearby where you may enjoy fantastic scenery.

B: OK, I will go for that.

A: Don't forget to take your helmet at any time when you riding a bike.

B: Thanks, I will do that.

Dialogue 3:

(substitute: kids club, fitness center, facilities, etc.)

______________________________________________

______________________________________________

______________________________________________

______________________________________________

# 6. Tips of Applying for Visa

**Pre – class Learning:** Watch the video and learn how to apply for Visa, then finish the following tasks.

**Topic:** Think about it and share your opinions on the online forum.

1. Do you know what travel visa is? What is it used for?
   (cues: enter into another country, grant, permission, etc.)
2. How many types of visa do embassy or consulate issue?
   (cues: short – stay or visit visa, long – stay visa, electronic visa, etc.)

**Test:** Please watch the video online and fill out the form below.

Please identify the information on the following picture.

VISA UNITED STATES OF AMERICA

| | | |
|---|---|---|
| Issuing Post Name | | |
| GUANGZHOU | | Nationality |
| Surname LI | | CHIN |
| Given Name HUA | | Visa Type/Class |
| Passport Number: xxxxx | | B1/B2 |
| Entries | Issue Date | Expiration Date |
| 1 | 16AUG2006 | 15NOV2006 |

1. From the picture, we can see this Visa allows entry for ________ time.
2. This Visa is expired at the date of ________ .
3. This Visa is issued at the place ________ .
4. This Visa type is ________.

### Wordlist

Glossary

| | | | |
|---|---|---|---|
| emigrate | 移居外国 | embassy | 大使馆 |
| consulate | 领事馆 | schengen area | 申根地区 |
| issue | 签发 | grant | 允许/授予 |
| visa – free zone | 免签地区 | on – arrival visa | 落地签 |

续表

| transit visa | 过境签 | immigration visa | 移民签证 |
|---|---|---|---|
| electronic visa | 电子签证 | visitor visa | 旅游签证 |
| long – stay visa | 长期停留签证 | official visa | 公务签证 |

## In – class Learning

### Skill Tips

*Background information of Visa*

*What is Visa*: A visa generally gives non – citizens permission to appear at a foreign port of entry to apply for admission to a foreign country and to remain there within specified constraints, such as a time frame for entry, a limit on the time spent in the country, and a prohibition against employment.

A visa application in advance of arrival gives the country a chance to consider the applicant's circumstances, such as financial security, reason for travelling, and details of previous visits to the country. A visitor may also be required to undergo and pass security or health checks upon arrival at the port of entry.

*Types of Visa*

By purpose:

- Transit visa
- Short – stay or visitor visa
- Long – stay visa
- Immigrant visa
- Official visa

By method of issue:

- On – arrival visa
- Electronic visa

## Reading Text

What is the Purpose of a Passport and Visa for International Travel?

When travelling between different countries, a passport is required to gain access and cross the country's borders. The purpose of a passport is to show other nations that you are a legal citizen of your particular nation of origin. For example, if you are American and want to enter the United Kingdom, you must show customs your passport in the United Kingdom to prove that you are a U. S. citizen before they will allow you entry. Essentially, a passport asks other nations permission for you to cross their borders, even if it is temporary. Most passports contain your photograph, name and birth date, along with your nation of origin and a signature. American passports typically last for ten years, and the expiration date is clearly shown on the inside cover. Every country has specific guidelines in terms of getting a passport.

Visas are another document designed to allow people access into other countries. The difference between a visa and a passport is: a visa specifies certain reasons why that person will be staying in the country. It also specifies a certain time frame. It is really a supplement to the passport, since both are required at the same time. The visa is usually stapled or attached to the passport and shown at the time of entry into another country. Most visas have time limits, and typically that time extends to about six months.

Passports are a form of legitimate identity, mainly because of the procedure that people must follow in order to get one. Most countries require an original birth certificate as proof of citizenship and identification. There is also a fee and a waiting period, along with other requirements. This process ensures that people applying are able to supply positive identification. The true reason behind passports and visas are to protect the people living in their native countries from foreigners who may be terrorists or illegal immigrants that cannot provide proof of their national origin. It can be considered a global identification system, since they are used in just about every country in the world. Passports and visas keep us safe and allow us to see and travel the world.

(adapted from website http://www.travelinsurancereview.net/2010/02/23/what-is-the-purpose-of-a-passport-and-visa-for-international-travel/)

Question 1: What is purpose of passport?

Question 2: How long does American passport typically last?

Question 3: What is the difference between passport and visa?

Question 4: What is the true reason behind passport and visa?

## Project

Let us find the process of how to apply for the American Visa. Follow the steps.

Step 1: Visit website http://www.ustraveldocs.com/cn/cn-niv-visaapply.asp and read the details of how to apply for an American visa.

Step 2: Please tell us the process of how to apply for the American Visa.

Step 3: Try to fill out your personal DS-160 https://ceac.state.gov/genniv/ and then present it in the class.

**U. S. ELECTRONIC APPLICATION CENTER**

Applying For a Nonimmigrant Visa

Personal information

Surname ______ Given name ______

Full name in native alphabet ______

Sex: Male ○ Female ○

Marital Status

Married○ Common law marriage ○Civil union/Domestic partnership ○ Single ○

Widowed ○ Divorced ○ Legally separated ○ Other○

Date and place of birth

Date ______ (Format: DD-MM-YYYY)

City ______ State/Province ______ Country/Region ______

National identification number ______

Address and phone information

Home address

Street ______ City ______ State/Province ______ Country ______

Passport/Travel type

Regular○ Official ○ Diplomatic ○ Laissez-passer ○ Other ○

Where was the passport/travel document issued?

City ______ State/Province* ______ if shown on passport Country/Region ______

Issuance date (Format: DD-MM-YYYY) ________

Expiration date (Format: DD-MM-YYYY) ________

Step 4：Suppose you are an exchange student in the Unites States. Design a dialogue between the interviewer and you. Think about what questions the interviewer will ask and how you will answer these questions.

Dialogue：

（cues：stay time，accommodation，purpose，etc.）

______________________________________________________________

______________________________________________________________

______________________________________________________________

______________________________________________________________

# Unit 4 Shopping and Food

## Learning Objectives

You are going to learn the following skills that are necessary for your daily life.

- ➢ You will learn to shop online.
- ➢ You will learn ways to argue with the salesman.
- ➢ You will learn to purchase with reasonable price.
- ➢ You will learn to order fast food.
- ➢ You will learn to eat western food at restaurant.
- ➢ You will learn to choose healthy food at supermarket.

## 1. Online Shopping

**Pre – class Learning:** Watch the video and learn how to shop online, then finish the following tasks.

**Topic:** Think about it and share your opinions on the online forum.

1. Why do so many people choose to purchase online? What kinds of goods will they buy online?
   (cues: scientific supplies, health, beauty, fashion, books, cellphones and accessories, etc.)
2. What factor affects your decision when you shop online?
   (cues: shipping rate, price, refund & return policy, seller information, product description, etc.)

**Test:** Please watch the video online and answer the questions in the form.

| Please answer the following questions according to what you have learned from the video. |
| --- |
| 1. What basic sales information have been mentioned in the video? |
| 2. If there is no goods available, how would you describe the stock? |
| 3. If your order reaches a certain amount of money, then you are entitled not to pay any shipping rate, what is this shipping condition called? |
| 4. Which two evaluation methods have been mentioned in the video? |

## Wordlist

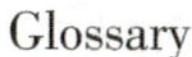

Glossary

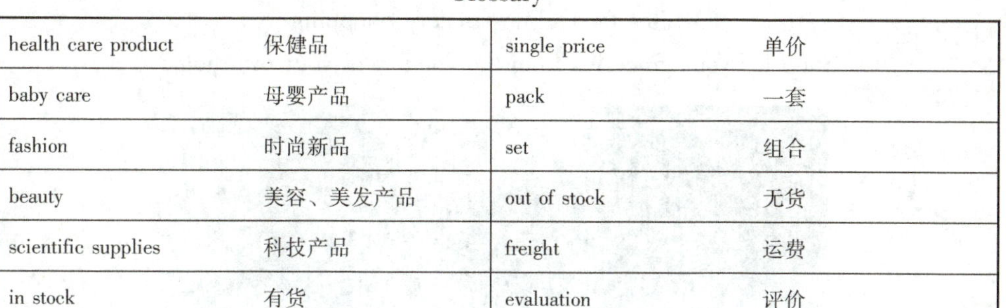

| health care product | 保健品 | single price | 单价 |
|---|---|---|---|
| baby care | 母婴产品 | pack | 一套 |
| fashion | 时尚新品 | set | 组合 |
| beauty | 美容、美发产品 | out of stock | 无货 |
| scientific supplies | 科技产品 | freight | 运费 |
| in stock | 有货 | evaluation | 评价 |

## In – class Learning

### Skill Tips

*Something you have to know when shopping online*:

- Product description includes brief introduction and detail information.
- Price may be a single price or a pack/set price. If you want to know the single price of some item, you should check price per piece.
- There are three terms to describe the number of items available in the stock. Normally it's described as in stock, out of stock, and × (number) left in stock.
- There are three types of sellers available on Amazon: Amazon's shop, joint shop, third – party shop.
- Shipping freight varies under different conditions. The products you buy may be eligible for free shipping, conditional free shipping or they may have shipping charges attached.
- Reviews from previous customers or for seller are useful for your choice.

**Reading Text**

3 Sites for Online Grocery Shopping

Shop for your groceries from the comfort of your own home

A growing number of supermarkets allow their customers to shop online for their groceries, preparing the order for pick – up or delivering it directly to their door. Shopping from home for your grocery store items is a great way to deal with this necessary chore: it's convenient, it's a time saver, and sometimes you can even take advantage of online sales not otherwise accessible. Here we will introduce three sites for online grocery shopping:

01 *Amazon Grocery Lets You Subscribe for Easy Orders*

*Amazon* is the largest online retailer today. The company's grocery offerings span from beverages to meats to seasonal gifts and baskets.

In the past few years, *Amazon* has greatly expanded its online grocery items, offering subscriptions to frequently purchased items.

If you subscribe to regular delivery (every one, two, three, or four months), you can save a significant amount of money. Use a Dash button for re – ordering—it's free and streamlines the purchase of frequently used items.

Amazon Prime customers enjoy free shipping on all grocery orders that qualify for this offer, as well as any discounts additional that might apply.

02 *Fresh Direct Specializes in Kosher, Gluten – Free, and Organic Foods*

Fresh Direct delivers fresh, organic, gourmet food to many different areas within the United States. Just enter your zip code to find out if they deliver to your area.

Their online grocery items come directly from local farms and dairies, with specialization for people with kosher, gluten – free, or organic and natural food preferences.

03 *Local Harvest Connects You with Seasonal, Fresh Foods*

Local Harvest aims to connect people in their local communities with fresh, organic, farm – to – table produce and goods. Customers can find produce online both in their local areas and other cities nationwide; not all of the farms represented in their directory offer delivery outside of their local areas, but many do.

Shoppers can also take advantage of community supported agriculture deliveries, subscribing to seasonal produce and visiting their selected farms once each season.

(adapted from https://www.lifewire.com/groceries – online – 3482646)

Question 1: How do you save a significant amount of money if you buy grocery on *Amazon*?

Question 2: Do Amazon Prime customers need to pay shipping rate for all grocery orders?

Question 3: Which grocery offer items for people with special needs?

Question 4: What is Local Harvest's specialty?

## Project

Let us find sales information on Amazon.com.

Step 1: Pick one of the following best sellers and fill out their sales information. (cues: beauty, scientific supplies, health, baby care, fashion, appliance, etc.)

| Goods | Description | Price | Stock | Seller Information | Shipping Freight | Evaluation |
|---|---|---|---|---|---|---|
| | | | | | | |

Step 2: Enter the website address https://www.amazon.com/gp/offer – listing/B01JZD2STI/ref = dp_olp_all_mbc? ie = UTF8&condition = all. Read the following five buying options for this car seat and circle your ideal one after filling up the form.

**Chicco KidFit 2-in-1 Belt-Positioning Booster Car Seat, Wimbledon**
by Chicco
186 customer reviews | Share
Color: **Wimbledon**
Lowest offer for each

Refine by Clear all
Shipping
prime
Free shipping
Condition
New
Open Box
Like New
Very Good
Good
Acceptable

| Price + Shipping | Condition (Learn more) | Delivery | Seller Information | Buying Options |
|---|---|---|---|---|
| $86.99 prime<br>& FREE Shipping<br>Details | Open Box - Like New<br>Item will come in original packaging. Packaging will be damaged. | FULFILLMENT BY AMAZON<br>· Shipping rates and return policy. | amazon warehouse | Add to cart |
| $99.99 prime<br>& FREE Shipping<br>Details | New | · Shipping rates and return policy. | amazon.com | Add to cart |
| $127.99<br>& FREE Shipping | New | · Ships from NY, United States.<br>· Shipping rates and return policy. | Global Supplies NY<br>94% positive over the past 12 months. (30,927 | Add to cart |
| $129.11<br>& FREE Shipping | New | · Ships from GA, United States.<br>· Shipping rates and return policy. | First Choice Department Store<br>96% positive over the past 12 months. (1,830 total ratings) | Add to cart |
| $130.46<br>& FREE Shipping | New | · Ships from FL, United States.<br>· Shipping rates and return policy. | JWD Products<br>82% positive over the past 12 months. (1,861 total ratings) | Add to cart |

| | Single Price | Shipping Rate | Tax | Seller | Shipper | Customer Rating |
|---|---|---|---|---|---|---|
| Option One | | | | | | |
| Option Two | | | | | | |
| Option Three | | | | | | |
| Option Four | | | | | | |
| Option Five | | | | | | |

## 2. Communicate with the Salesman

**Pre - class Learning:** Watch the video and learn how to communicate with salesman, then finish the following tasks.

**Topic:** Think about it and share your opinions on the online forum.

1. Did you have any experience on returning or replacing goods when you shop online? If yes, why would you do that?
   (cues: better price available, wrong size/pattern/color/style/product, broken item, quality problem, etc.)
2. Which way would you choose to contact customer service if you meet problems when you shop online and why?
   (cues: email, telephone, online chat, etc.)

**Test:** Please watch the video online and finish the task required.

Please answer the following questions according to what you have learned from the video.

1. Which information will you pay attention to when viewing the order details?

2. After your goods is delivered from oversea, what will you submit in order to get custom clearance?

3. If you have problems with your goods, what will you do?

**Wordlist**

Glossary

| | | | |
|---|---|---|---|
| track | 追踪 | confirmation | 确认 |
| import | 进口 | deposit | 押金 |
| status | 状态 | charged | 已收费 |
| summary | 总结 | subtotal | 汇总 |
| package | 包裹 | submit | 提交 |
| return | 退货 | replace | 换货 |
| resolve | 解决 | feedback | 反馈 |
| review | 评论 | check out | 结账 |

## In - class Learning

### Skill Tips

*Useful expressions in after sale service*

Making complaints

- I found my new purchased ××× from your shop doesn't work now.
- I bought ××× from your shop yesterday, but I found it fail to work now.
- My newly bought ××× seriously lose color after laundry.
- Can I get a refund or exchange for the wrong product?
- Can I return the extra if I buy too much of this item?
- I didn't find the return or refund policy of your goods.
- This product is past its expiration date.
- How much do you charge after warranty period?

After sale service

- What is your order number?
- If your product is still in the warranty period, we provide free maintenance.
- Within 30 days of receipt, you are allowed to exchange or return your goods without usage.
- Sorry, you can't exchange your product because it is already used.

### Reading Text

Returns Policy and Refunds of Tesco

*Is your item faulty or damaged?*

We do our best to make sure everything works perfectly, but if you find that any of our products are faulty within 12 months from purchase, we guarantee you a full refund, repair or replacement.

Many electrical or mobile phone problems can be resolved quickly by our product support guides or by our helplines.

Visit our product support page and get step - by - step instructions, trouble - shooter tips and FAQs on selected products.

If that doesn't solve your problem, contact the helpline on 0800 323 4060 (or 0330 123 4060 local rate from a mobile).

All items we supply are required to comply with the contract. If they don't, you have the following rights in addition to your legal rights.

1. Within 30 days of receipt of the goods (or for perishable goods within their use - by date), you will be offered the choice of a repair or full refund.

2. From 30 days after receipt of the goods until 12 months, we will arrange for a repair of the goods and, if this does not work, a refund.

3. After the first 12 months from receipt of the goods, you may be offered a partial refund or repair, depending on the product and usage.

Alternatively, our Customer Service team are here to help, you can reach them on 0800 323 4050 (or 0330 123 4050 local rate from a mobile).

Where possible, damage in transit should be notified within 48 hours of receipt of the goods, by contacting the Customer Service helpline on 0800 323 4050 (or 0330 123 4050 local rate from a mobile).

We reserve the right to send out an engineer or technician to inspect the goods to confirm the fault before accepting the return.

If you have any complaints about an online transaction, please get in touch at our Contact US page and we will endeavor to find a solution. If you would like to escalate your complaint, the European Commission has set up an online service to resolve disputes about online transactions. Please visit the online dispute resolution website.

(adapted from website https://www.tesco.com/help/returns-policy/)

Question 1: How long will the Tesco guarantee you a full refund, repair or replacement, if your item is damaged or faulty?

Question 2: After the first 12 months from receipt of the goods, what will you get according to returns policy?

Question 3: If the goods got damaged in transit, what would you do?

Question 4: If you are not satisfied with the solution for faulty online purchase, what could you do?

## Project

Work with your partner by designing a dialogue in the following situation and act it out in the class.

Step 1: Enter website https://www. tesco. com/help/returns – policy/ and find more details of returns policy.

Step 2: Design a dialogue in the following situation.

| Situation: You bought a bottle of Neutrogena Alcohol and Oil – free Toner at an online store, but you found the bottle cap was broken and it was leaking. Call the Customer Service to report this problem and try to find a solution you feel satisfied with. You may use the expressions listed on the skill tips. |
| --- |

Dialogue 1:

________________________________________

________________________________________

________________________________________

________________________________________

# 3. Tips of Money Saving

**Pre－class Learning:** Watch the video and learn how to save the money, then finish the following tasks.

**Topic:** Think about it and share your opinions on the online forum.

1. If you want to have a bargain, where will you go in your city?
   (cues: market, street vendors, fair, etc. )
2. Do you have some skills of finding goods with good quality and reasonable price? Please share with us.
   (cues: website, yard sale, charity sale, warehouse store, etc. )

**Test:** Please watch the video online and fill out the form below.

| Please answer the following questions according to what you have learned from the video. |
|---|
| 1. Where could you go if you want to buy second－hand goods with reasonable price? |
| 2. If you are a member of Amazon Prime, what advantage could you make of in lightning deals? |
| 3. Do second－hand products come with warranty? |
| 4. What is the meaning of GVP? |

**Wordlist**

Glossary

| yard sale | 后院大甩卖 | church sale | 教堂甩卖 |
|---|---|---|---|
| community sale | 社区甩卖 | consignment store | 二手商店 |
| thrift store | 二手商店 | cash back | 返还现金 |
| clearance | 清仓 | warranty | 保证 |

## In – class Learning

### Skill Tips

*Places where you can bargain*

outdoor fair

yard sale

market

consignment store

*Sales season or public holidays in the west*

New Year's Day

St. Valentine's Day

National day

Easter Day

Black Friday/Thanksgiving Day

Boxing Day/Christmas day

## Reading Text

How to Haggle: Tips for Bargaining Overseas

By RickSteve's

In much of the Mediterranean world, the price tag is only an excuse to argue. Bargaining is the accepted and expected method of finding a compromise between the wishful thinking of the merchant and the tourist. You can generally fight prices at flea markets, touristy souvenir shops, and with street vendors, but not at modern stores or shopping malls.

Here are a few guidelines to help you get the best bargain:

Determine if bargaining is appropriate. It is bad shopping etiquette to "make an offer" in a London department store. It's foolish not to do at a Greek flea market. To learn if a price is fixed, show some interest in an item but say, "It's just too much money." You've put the merchant in a position to make the first offer. If he comes down even 2 percent, there's nothing sacred about the price tag. Haggle away.

Shop around to find out what locals pay. Prices can vary drastically among vendors at the same flea market, and even at the same stall. If prices aren't posted, assume there's a double price standard: one for locals and one for you. If only tourists buy the item you're pricing, see what an Arab, Spanish, or Italian tourist would be charged. I remember thinking I did well in Istanbul's Grand Bazaar, until I learned my Spanish friend bought the same shirt for 30 percent less.

Determine the merchant's lowest price. Merchants hate to lose a sale. Work the cost down, but if it doesn't match with the price you have in mind, walk away. That last amount the merchant hollers out as you turn the corner is often the best price you'll get. If that price is right, go back and buy. Prices often drop at the end of the day, when merchants are about to pack up.

Curb your enthusiasm. As soon as the merchant perceives the "I got to have that!" in you, you'll never get the best price.

Ask for a deal on multiple items. See if the merchant will give you a better price if you buy in bulk (three necklaces instead of one). The more they think they can sell, the more flexible they may become.

Offer to pay cash at stalls that take credit cards. You can expect to pay cash for most things at street markets, but some merchants who sell pricier goods (nice jewelry, artwork, etc.) take credit cards, too. They're often more willing to strike a deal if you pay cash, since they don't lose any profit to credit – card fees.

(adapted from https://www.ricksteves.com/travel-tips/money/how-to-haggle)

Question 1: Can you bargain at a flea market?

Question 2: How to check if the price in tag is negotiable?

Question 3: Is it true that the price is fixed at the same vendor?

Question 4: Will you get the best price if you say "I got to have that"?

**Project**

Let us start to bargain under different situations.

Situation 1: Summer break is on the corner, you are purchasing clothes for your holiday trip. The first choice is to purchase on the Internet. Could you please tell us how many ways you may use to get the best price? Design a dialogue of talking about what you have bought on the amazon. com with your friend Jane.

Model dialogue

A: Hi, Jane, do you have any plan for summer holiday?

B: Not yet. How about you?

A: I will go to the beach so I am thinking about what to wear on the beach.

B: Why don't you shop online because a lot of online – shops will have summer sales recently?

A: Yes, it is true. I have already bought a sunhat and a pair of sunglasses on *Amazon*.

B: Great! Did you get any discount?

A: Yes, I do. I use coupon to get 35% discount and what's more, it is free shipping.

B: Excellent!

Dialogue 1:
(substitute: items, discount, shipping condition, etc.)

______________________________________________

______________________________________________

______________________________________________

______________________________________________

Situation 2: You are deciding to go out to get more choices of bargains. First, you will go to the shopping center at downtown. Could you please tell us how many ways the shopping centers will use to market their goods? Design a dialogue between a salesman and you.

Model dialogue
A: Hello, what can I help you?
B: Yes, do you have any promotion here?
A: Yes, we do have summer sales here. All goods with yellow tags are on sale now. You may check it here, here and there.
B: Do the clothes on that rack all have 50% discount?
A: Yes, they do. And if you purchase three clothes all together, you will get additional 25% discount.
B: Great!

Dialogue 2:
(substitute: items, discount, etc.)

______________________________________________

______________________________________________

______________________________________________

______________________________________________

Situation 3: Now, you are considering yard sale would be a good place to bargain. Design a dialogue that you bargain with the goods owner.

Model dialogue
A: Hi, how much is this toy?
B: Five dollars.
A: How about 2?
B: No, it is almost a new toy which is a fantastic choice for the kid.
A: Well, how about 3? It is the reasonable price for a used kid toy.
B: OK, deal is done.

Dialogue 3:

(substitute: items, discount, shipping condition, etc.)

______________________________________________

______________________________________________

______________________________________________

______________________________________________

# 4. Order Fast Food

**Pre – class Learning:** Watch the video and learn how to order fast food abroad, then finish the following tasks.

**Topic:** Think about it and share your opinions on the online forum.

1. Can you name some worldwide fast food restaurants?
   (cues: burger king, subway, McDonald's, etc.)
2. Do you like fast food? Why do modern people like to order fast food?
   (cues: tasty, convenient, clean environment, etc.)

**Test:** Please watch the video online and answer the questions below.

Please answer the following questions according to what you have learned from the video.

1. America is called a country on the wheel. So if you want to buy fast food without getting off the car, where could you buy the food?

2. If you are veggie, what kind of burger will you order at McDonald's?

3. What is the difference between chicken burger and chicken burger meal?

4. How many sizes of cups in Starbucks?

**Wordlist**

Glossary

| eat in | 堂食 | take away | 外卖 |
|---|---|---|---|
| meal | 套餐 | nugget | 鸡块 |
| wings | 鸡翅 | veggie | 素食 |
| topping | 配料 | sides | 小点 |
| decaf | 去咖啡因的 | syrup | 糖浆 |
| whipped | 奶油 | vanilla | 香草 |
| caramel | 焦糖 | hazelnut | 榛子 |

## In – class Learning

### Skill Tips

*Top* 10 *best fast food restaurants*

1. McDonald's 2. Pizza Hut 3. KFC 4. Domino's Pizza
5. Burger King 6. Starbucks 7. Subway 8. Dunkin' Donuts
9. Dairy Queen 10. Papa Johns

### Reading Text

The History of Fast Food in America

The history of fast food in America runs parallel to the invention of the car. These two industries are so intertwined that most people today think of fast food as anything being served out of a window and into an automobile. McDonald's can easily claim fame for perfecting the service and style of cooking we know today as fast food but the first fast food restaurant in the U. S. was not a McDonald's. It was White Castle, a hamburger joint that opened in Wichita, Kansas, in 1916.

Curb service, where a fast food restaurant employee delivers food from the restaurant to waiting customers outside in their cars, started as a novelty in the 1920s but was so popular the practice spread nationwide in short order. By the 1940s, the friendly carshop person delivering the food to the cars had gone mobile, too, wearing roller skates to speed service. Drive – through windows soon followed.

Burgers and fries used to be the main stay of the industry but today's fast food menu offerings are much more eclectic than ever before. Some of the most popular of the new fast food offerings include pizza, chicken nuggets, specialty sandwiches, hot dogs, onion rings, and even ice cream and cupcakes.

The fast food industry in the U. S. has embraced ethnic food trends, too, making tacos, Vietnamese noodles, kebabs, egg rolls, fried rice, sushi, and bento baskets menu items in high demand. Coffee shops serve up beverages prepared and smoothies are a fast food beverage option that caters to the health – conscious crowd.

Fast food is everywhere. Street vendors, food trucks, delivery services, sports arenas, and even convenience stores and gas stations all sell food that can be bought quickly, cheaply, and eaten on the fly. We've become such a fast food nation that the once – traditional, sit – down dining experience presented in slower, more formal style is often reserved for special occasions.

(adapted from https://www.accupos.com/pos-articles/history-of-fast-food-in-america/)

Question 1: When was the first fast food restaurant open in the U. S. ?

Question 2: What food used to be the mainstay of the industry?

Question 3: Does fast food industry in the U. S. now offer ethnic food now?

Question 4: According to author, when will American people choose to sit down and experience a more formal style of dinning?

## Project

Let us make orders at different fast food stores.

Situation 1: You are at the coffee bar with your friend Mike. Please help your friend Mike order a cup of coffee. First please review the process of ordering a coffee and then make a dialogue.

| Model dialogue |
|---|
| A: Hi, how are you doing? |
| B: Fine, thanks. I'd like to get a venti café mocha with whip please. |
| A: Did you say with or without whip? |
| B: With whipped. |
| A: Got it. What's your name? |
| B: Kate. |
| A: Got it. That will be five seventeen. |
| B: Here you go. Thanks. |

Dialogue 1:

(substitute: size, extra needs, cost, etc.)

________________________________________

________________________________________

________________________________________

Situation 2: You are driving on the way to the beach. Now you are a bit hungry, and plan to get some fast food at McDonald's. Please make a dialogue of ordering fast food.

| Model dialogue |
|---|
| A: Welcome to McDonald's. Can I take your order please? |
| B: Could I have a big mac meal with 4 pieces of chicken wings? |
| A: Sure. What do you want for drink? |
| B: Coke, please. |
| A: Do you want normal size or large size? |
| B: Normal size. |
| A: Are you eating in or taking away? |
| A: Eating in. |
| B: That will be 5 dollars. |

Dialogue 2:

(substitute: items, cost, deliver method, etc.)

________________________________________

________________________________________

________________________________________

## 5. Eat at Restaurant

**Pre - class Learning:** Watch the video and learn how to eat at restaurant, then finish the following tasks.

**Topic:** Think about it and share your opinions on the online forum.

1. How do you order food in a typical Chinese - style restaurant?

   (cues: menu, hot dishes, cold dishes, etc.)

2. Can you tell the difference of table manners between Chinese and western culture?

   (cues: serving order, environment, eating etiquette, etc.)

**Test:** Please watch the video online and fill out the form below.

Please answer the following questions according to what you have learned from the video.

1. What two styles of dinning does the author introduce?

2. What style of dinning will switch fork and knife?

3. What is the only time that the European style of dinning puts down the knife?

### Wordlist

Glossary

| | | | |
|---|---|---|---|
| fork | 叉子 | switch | 变换 |
| knife | 刀子 | spoon | 汤勺 |
| etiquette | 礼仪 | implement | 操作 |
| utensil | 器具 | placement | 放置 |
| course | 一道菜 | grip | 抓握 |

## In – class Learning

### Skill Tips

*The following picture shows the basic table setting*

*About silence service code on western table*

| I do not finish this course. | I completely finish this course. | I do not finish this course. |
|---|---|---|

### Reading Text

Impress Your Friends by Ordering Food in English at a Restaurant

Everyone likes eating out at restaurants. When you are in an English – speaking country, knowing how to order correctly can impress your friends and make the difference between an average and an amazing dining experience. Ordering food in English at a restaurant is easy, too—if you follow these simple tips.

*Get the right table*

Book a table on the phone or ask for a table by saying "We'd like a table for 5, please." This will let the waiter know how many people to expect. The waiter might ask "How many people are in your party?" In this question "party" means "group" not "celebration". If you're in a country where people are allowed to smoke in restaurants, the waiter might ask if you'd like to sit in the smoking or non – smoking section. If you're in a hot country, the waiter may ask if you'd prefer to sit indoors or outdoors. Make it clear exactly where you want to sit for a perfect meal.

*Order food*

When the waiter asks "Are you ready to order?" or "Can I take your order?" if you are ready, you can give your order. Use "I'd like..." or "I'll have..." to introduce your order and expression "for starter/appetizer" to talk about the first course and "for main course" to talk about the second course of food you will eat.

If you are not sure what to order, ask the waiter "What would you recommend?" to get some advice or "What are the specialties?" to find out what the most famous dishes are at that restaurant. You could also ask "What are today's specials?" to find out if there are any dishes being served today that are not usually on the menu.

If you want to order wine with your main course, you can use the waiter's expert knowledge to help choose something great. Ask the waiter "What wine goes well with this?" or "What wine matches this?" to make sure they taste great together.

*Pay the bill*

Catch the waiter's attention and ask "Can we have the bill, please?" or "Check, please." to see how much you need to pay. The waiter might ask if you want to pay separately or as a group. Check the bill to see if a service charge or tip has been added. This is money that is given to the waiting staff for good service. If this hasn't been added, it's common in most English speaking countries to leave some extra money (usually 10% – 15% of the bill) for the waiter.

So, now you know how to order food at a restaurant in English, all that's left to do is enjoy your food and have a great time!

(adapted from https://englishlive.ef.com/blog/english – in – the – real – world/impress – friends – ordering – food – english – restaurant/)

Question 1: What does "party" in the sentence of "How many people are in your party?" mean?

Question 2: If you have no idea of what to order, what would you say?

Question 3: If you are not an expert for the wine, what would you do when ordering wine with your main course?

Question 4: How much tips should you leave in most English speaking countries?

**Project**

Let us order a dinner at a restaurant.

Step 1: The following is a menu of a bistro. Let us see what is on the menu.

lite bites 轻食
platter 大盘菜
lasagna 意大利千层面
rib eye 牛脊肉
nachos 墨西哥烤玉米片
fajitas 墨西哥薄饼
tart 果酱饼
main course 主菜
sides 配菜

ROBINSONS BARS
EST 1895
BTI · SALOON · FIBBERS · BISTRO · ROXY

BISTRO EVENING MENU

LITE BITES

Selection of Breads .......... £4
With butter, tapenade & oils

Chef's Soup of the Day .......... £4
With a crusty roll

Potato & Leek Soup .......... £4
With a crusty roll

Breaded Mushrooms .......... £5
With a roast garlic & herb mayonnaise

Cajun Blackened Chicken Wings .......... £6
With sweet chilli glaze & cucumber dip

Prawn Cocktail .......... £6
With marie-rose sauce

Cheesy Garlic Bread .......... £4

Bruschetta .......... £5
Topped with sun dried tomato, basil & Oakwood cheddar

Chicken Caesar Salad .......... £6
With bacon & parmesan

Spicy Nachos .......... £5
Topped with salsa, jalapeños, cheese & sour cream

ROBINSONS PLATTER FOR 2
£10
Mushrooms, chicken wings, garlic bread & nachos, with garlic mayo & sweet chilli dips

MAIN COURSES

Pork & Leek Sausages .......... £10
With champ & roast onion gravy

Steak & Guinness Pie .......... £12
Topped with puff pastry & served with vegetables & chunky chips

Homemade Lasagne .......... £10
With chunky chips

Peppered Pork Chops .......... £11
With a warm salad of chorizo, spinach & baby potatoes

Chicken Goujons .......... £10
With chunky chips & sweet chilli sauce

Malaysian Chicken Curry .......... £12
With saffron rice & prawn crackers

Chicken Fajitas .......... £12
Wok-charred chicken fillet strips with peppers & onions. Served with salsa, jalapeños, sour cream, grated cheddar & flour tortillas
Vegetarian Option .......... £10

Bistro Burger .......... £10
On a floury bap, topped with Oakwood cheese & homemade relish, served with chunky chips

Beer Battered Cod & Chips .......... £11
With mushy peas & homemade tartare sauce

Cajun Chicken Fillet Burger .......... £11
On a floury bap, topped with Oakwood cheese & BBQ sauce, served with chunky chips

Sun Dried Tomato, Black Olive & Basil Tagliatelle .......... £10
With garlic bread
Add Chicken .......... £12

Steak Sandwich .......... £14
On ciabatta with mushrooms, onions & peppered sauce, served with chips

Pan Fried Chicken Fillet .......... £12
With pepper sauce & herb crushed potatoes

Caramelised Red Onion, Cranberry & Brie Tart .......... £10
With salad & chunky chips

10oz Dry Aged Ribeye .......... £18
With pepper sauce, crispy onion laces & chunky chips

Beef Shepherd's Pie .......... £10
Our twist on a classic! Topped with traditional champ

Baked Salmon Fillet .......... £12
With a bacon & leek cream sauce, served with mashed potato

SIDES

Mashed Root Vegetables .......... £3
Chips .......... £3
Garlic Potatoes .......... £3
Champ .......... £3
Baby Potatoes .......... £3
Garlic Bread .......... £2
House Salad .......... £3
Coleslaw .......... £2
Sauce Boat .......... £2

If you have a food allergy or intolerance, please let us know before ordering as our menu descriptions do not include all ingredients. Full allergen information for food and drink is available, upon request.

Step 2: Now let us order our own dinner and make a dialouge with your partner according to the menu above.

Model dialogue 1

A: Hi, welcome to Robinsons Bars. How many people do you have?

B: Two.

A: Would you like a booth or a table?

B: I prefer a booth.

A: This way please. Here is your menu. (after a while) May I take your order now?

B: Yes, I would like steak & guinness pie, pan fried chicken fillet and house salad.

A: How would you like your steak cooked?

B: Medium well. (rare/medium/well done)

A: OK, what kind of dressing would you want with your salad?

B: Which dressing do you have?

A: We have got ranch dressing, thousand island, Italian, blue cheese and French dressing.

B: Ranch dressing, please.

A: Anything to drink?

B: Water is OK.

Model dialogue 2

A: Hello, do you have a reservation tonight?

B: Yes, I reserved a table under the name of Miller.

A: Well, let me check it. (after a few minutes) We do have the reservation for you. Please follow me to the table.

B: Thanks.

A: Here is the menu. Please let me know if you are ready to order.

B: Thanks. What are the specialities in your restaurant?

A: Well. Grilled pork ribs and pancakes are very popular in our restaurant.

B: What is the size for one serving of pork ribs?

A: It is enough for a meat lover. But if you like, you may add sides. We have salad, chips and onion rings.

B: Well, I would like a grilled pork rib and vegetable salad.

A: Would you like something to drink?

B: A bottle of coke, please.

Dialogue:

________________________________________

________________________________________

________________________________________

________________________________________

## 6. Oversea Supermarket

**Pre – class Learning**: Watch the video and learn how to find healthy food in the supermarket, then finish the following tasks.

**Topic**: Think about it and share your opinions on the online forum.

1. What kind of food do you think is healthy?
   (cues: grain, vegetable, fruit, etc.)
2. Can you tell us some skills to find healthy food in the supermarket? What are they?
   (cues: free range egg, organic food, non – GMO food, etc.)

**Test**: Please watch the video online and fill out the form below.

| Please answer the following questions according to what you have learned from the video. |
|---|
| 1. Which one is healthier, white bread or grain bread? |
| 2. Which one is healthier, free range egg or caged egg? |
| 3. If you are allergic to gluten, what sign on the goods package should you pay attention to? |

### Wordlist

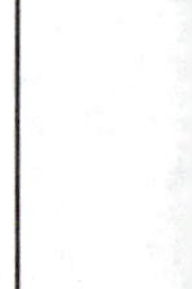

Glossary

| grocery | 杂货店 | deli | 熟食店 |
|---|---|---|---|
| bakery | 烘焙店 | bulk | 散装 |
| whole wheat | 全麦 | grain | 谷物 |
| gluten free | 无麸质 | organic | 有机的 |
| dairy free | 无乳糖 | liquor | 卖酒的店 |

## In – class Learning

### Skill Tips

*Knowledge about the meaning of different signs on the packaging.*

Gluten–Free Products

Dairy–Free Products

Organic Food

Non-GMO Food

### Reading Text

Nutritional Guidelines for Teens

By Jill Corleone, RDN, LD; Updated April 18, 2017

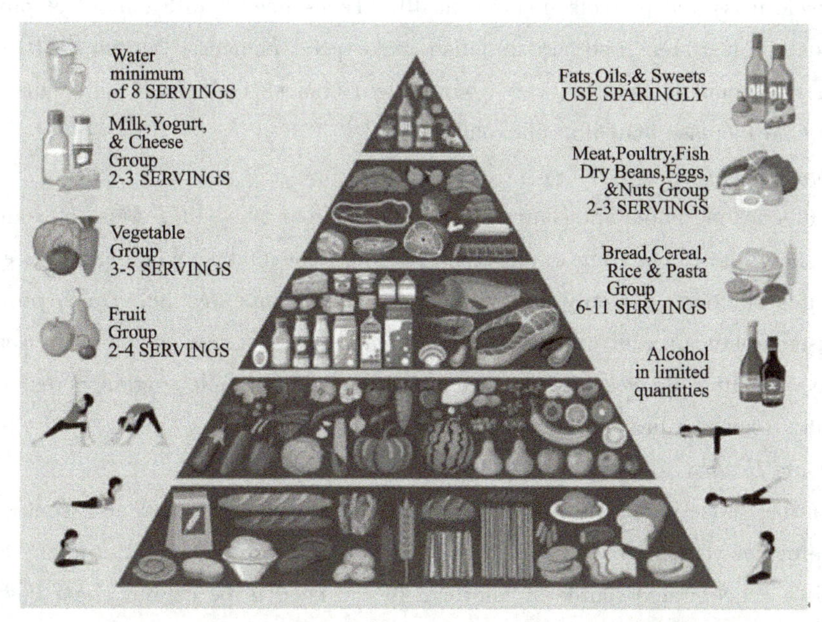

More than 17 percent of teens between the ages of 12 and 19 are overweight, according to the Weight – Control Information Network. Carrying more weight than your body needs increases your risk of developing adult like diseases, such as diabetes and heart disease, while you are still young. Restricting your intake, or dieting, is not the solution. Making changes to your diet by following healthy nutritional guidelines can help you feel better and improve your health now and later on.

*Fruits and Veggies Daily*

Make fruits and vegetables a part of your diet every day. Fruits and vegetables are low in calories and high in fiber and essential nutrients. The fiber in fruits and vegetables offers a number of health benefits. Fiber takes your body longer to digest, so it keeps you feeling full longer. Fiber also improves bowel function, preventing constipation.

*Calcium for Bone Health*

Getting enough calcium in your diet is especially important during your teen years because it helps promote bone health and strength. Teens need 1,300 milligrams of calcium a day. Milk is a good source of calcium with nearly 300 milligrams in an 8 – oz. serving of nonfat milk. Yogurt and cheese are also good sources of calcium. If you're not a fan of milk or dairy products, you can also get calcium from soy milk, tofu, and salmon with the bones and broccoli.

*The Power of Protein*

Adequate intakes of protein also support growth, along with helping to preserve lean muscle mass and promote immune health. Teens need 5 to 6 ounces of protein – rich foods a day. Meat, poultry and fish make good choices. But the 2010 dietary guidelines recommend that you vary your protein choices to include more nuts, seeds and beans to increase your nutrient intake.

*More Whole Grains*

Grains are an important source of energy for your busy life. Most of your grain choices should be whole grain to maximize your nutrient intake. Whole grains are also a good source of fiber. Not only does fiber help control appetite, but it also provides a more sustainable source of energy. Try to get at least 6 ounces of grains in your diet each day. Healthy choices include whole – grain bread, whole – grain cereal, brown rice, oats, whole – wheat pasta and popcorn.

*Choose Healthy Fats*

You may associate fat with weight gain, but fat in the diet is also an essential nutrient. It provides your body with energy and helps you absorb essential nutrients. However, fat is a concentrated source of calories, so you need to be careful about how much you eat each day.

(adapted from https://healthfully.com/485781-nutritional-guidelines-for-teens.html)

Question 1: What is the suggestion from the text to lose your weight?

Question 2: What is the function of fiber?

Question 3: If you're not a fan of milk or dairy products, what food can you get calcium from?

Question 4: Is it true that we should not intake any fat because we don't want gain weight?

## Project

Let us do role plays under different situations.

Situation 1: Suppose you are shopping in the supermarket but could not find items you need. Make a dialogue of asking salesman for help.

Model dialogue

A: Excuse me. Can you help me?

B: Sure. What can I do for you?

A: I am looking for cereals. Can you tell me where I can find cereals?

B: Which brand of cereals are you looking for?

A: I don't have any preference.

B: All major brands of cereals are on Aisle 3.

A: Thanks.

Dialogue 1:

(substitute: items, location, etc.)

__________________________________________

__________________________________________

__________________________________________

__________________________________________

__________________________________________

__________________________________________

Situation 2: Suppose you are asking more details of the goods in stock. Make a dialogue.

Model dialogue

A: Excuse me, I want to buy some canned tuna. But I see none displayed. Do you have more in stock?

B: I am not sure. Which brand do you prefer?

A: Any of them will do.

B: Let me check. Perhaps we have some brands in stock.

A: Will it take long?

B: Not at all, sir. Yes, we have some in Aisle 4. Look at the fourth row from right.

A: OK, thanks.

Dialogue 2:

(substitute: brand name, warranty, expiration date, origin, stock, etc.)

______________________________________________

______________________________________________

______________________________________________

______________________________________________

# Unit 5 Job Hunting

## Learning Objectives

You are going to learn the following skills that are necessary for your job hunting.

➢ You will learn ways to find a job.

➢ You will learn to write a cover letter and a resume which are essential for your job application.

➢ You will learn how to do the job interview.

➢ You will learn tips of job interview.

➢ You will learn job etiquette.

# 1. Find a Job Abroad

**Pre－class Learning:** Watch the video and learn how to find a job abroad, then finish the following tasks.

**Topic:** Think about it and share your opinions on the online forum.

1. List top three strengths that are essential for helping you find a good job.
   (cues: positive personality, team spirit, good communication skill, good listener, etc.)
2. Do you know what employability skill is and how to get these skills?
   (cues: communication skill, team work skill, planning and organization skill, etc.)

**Test:** Please watch the video online and answer the questions in the form.

| Please answer the following questions according to what you have learned from the video. |
|---|
| 1. What are the usual ways for people to find a job? |
| 2. What services or assistance can career center provide? |
| 3. What two categories of information are needed when searching for a job on indeed website? |

## Wordlist

Glossary

| | | | |
|---|---|---|---|
| graduate | 毕业生 | upload | 上传 |
| consultant | 顾问 | career center | 就业中心 |
| workshop | 学习班 | expertise | 专门知识 |
| flyer | 传单 | bulletin board | 公告栏 |

续表

| | | | |
|---|---|---|---|
| vacancy | 空缺 | resource | 资源 |
| zip code | 区号 | job title | 职位名称 |
| alert | 提醒 | salary | 薪水 |
| review | 评价 | subscription | 订阅 |
| rating | 等级 | benefit | 福利 |

## In – class Learning

### Skill Tips

*Sources of job information*:

- Recommendations from friends or relatives.
- Information from social network.
- Career page of local newspapers.
- Career websites or other online resources.
- Visit career center of your university.

*Functions of career center or career service of university*:

- Meet career consultant and get expertise advice in job hunting.
- Check job flyers on bulletin board on the campus.
- Take part in workshops to get work – related skills.
- Get access to numerous online resources on job vacancies.

### Reading Text

Marketing Your Way to Success

Marketing your way to success is simply selling yourself to a future employer. What can you offer this employer?

These across – job skills are called transferable skills because they are important to have in any occupation. The following skills are consistently identified as critical for anyone seeking to be successful in the 21st century world of work:

*Information and communication skills*

- Ability to communicate verbally with people inside and outside an organization

- Ability to communicate in writing
- Ability to obtain and process information
- Ability to create and/or edit written reports

*Thinking and problem – solving skills*

- Ability to make sound decisions and solve problems
- Ability to plan, organize and prioritize work
- Ability to analyze quantitative data
- Ability to think critically and creatively

*Interpersonal and self – directional skills*

- Ability to influence others
- Ability to work in a team structure
- Ability to demonstrate responsibility and self – discipline
- Display positive attitude and sense of self – worth
- Take responsibility for professional growth

*Technical skills*

- Technical knowledge related to the job
- Proficiency with computer software programs

These skills and qualities are strong marketing points and should be discussed in your resume, cover letter, and during the interview process. Consider which skills you already possess and which you want to strengthen.

The job interview is a key opportunity for marketing yourself to a potential employer. To prepare for an interview, write down some ideas for how you'll respond to one of the most frequently asked interview questions used by employers, "Why should I hire you?"

It helps if you can imagine a real situation so you can consider what the employer needs from you in order for their company to be successful. This is your chance to market yourself!

(adapted from https://www.calcareercenter.org/Home/Content? contentID = 131)

Question 1: What are cross – job skills called?

Question 2: According to the text, if you have a strong ability to influence others, what cross – job skills would you list on your resume?

Question 3: What skills and qualities should be strongly discussed in your resume and cover letter?

Question 4: To prepare for an interview, what question should you ask yourself in order to meet the employer's needs?

## Project

Let us do a job searching together.

Step 1: Enter website www. indeed. com and find a job you are interested.

Step 2: List the specifications of your targeted job below.

| Job title | Job type | Location | Responsibility | Requirement | Reviews | Salary |
|---|---|---|---|---|---|---|
| | | | | | | |

Step 3: Please fill out the blanks below and finish the self – assessment.

| What skills does this company require? | What technical skills do you employ? | What employability skills do you employ? | What is your interest on the job? | What is your expectation from the company? |
|---|---|---|---|---|
| | | | | |

Step 4: Let us make dialogues under different situations.

Situation 1: Suppose you discuss with a career consultant on preparations for applying for a job.

Model dialogue

A: Good afternoon, Mr. /Mrs. ...

B: Good afternoon, what can I do for you?

A: I'm interested in a position advertised on the bulletin board. But I don't know how to apply for it. Do I need to prepare anything for the application?

B: Of course, in order to leave a deep impression on your perspective employer, you could show your key skills in your resume.

A: I've no idea about it. Would you please explain it in details? What are the basic requirements?

B: Of course. I will list for you.

A: Many thanks.

B: My pleasure.

Dialogue 1:

( substitute: cover letter, resume, email, any advice from the career consultant, etc. )

______________________________________________

______________________________________________

______________________________________________

______________________________________________

Situation 2: Suppose there is a job vacancy in the company where your friend is working. You are interested in it, but before your application, you want to get more information about the company from your friend.

| Model dialogue |
| --- |
| A: Hey, are you still looking for a job recently? My company is recruiting a ... (position). |
| B: Really? That's so cool. |
| A: If you are interested in it, you should apply for it through our website. |
| B: How is your company? What is the core value of your company? |
| A: It encourages innovation and respects personal potentials. I love working there. |
| B: How are the benefits and welfare system? |
| A: We have a sound welfare system with 7 day's paid leave. |
| B: Sounds amazing. I will try to send my resume as soon as possible. Thanks for the news. |
| A: Pleasure. |

Dialogue 2:

(substitute: secretary, assistant manager , any questions related with the company, etc. )

______________________________________________

______________________________________________

______________________________________________

______________________________________________

## 2. Application Letter and Resume

**Pre - class Learning:** Watch the video and learn how to apply for a job, then finish the following tasks.

**Topic:** Think about it and share your opinions on the online forum.

1. Do you have any experience in taking a part - time job? Why or why not?
   (cues: lack of time, focus on study, worry about safety, parents' support, enrich college life, build confidence, etc.)
2. What's your dream job after graduation?
   (cues: good pay, major - related job, convenient transport, sound welfare system, excellent bonus, great potential for promotion, etc.)

**Test:** Please watch the video online and answer the questions in the form.

Please answer the following questions according to what you have learned from the video.

1. From the video, which three parts should be included in a complete job application?

2. What is the purpose of a cover letter?

3. Is it a good suggestion to write your job application as long as possible?

4. What is the aim of selection criteria?

**Wordlist**

Glossary

| profile | 简介 | recruiter | 招聘人员 |
|---|---|---|---|
| achievement | 成就 | nationality | 国籍 |
| criteria | 标准 | competence | 能力 |
| qualification | 资质 | highlight | 强调 |
| candidate | 候选人 | working experience | 工作经验 |

续表

| intermediate | 中级 | training | 培训 |
|---|---|---|---|
| management | 管理 | discipline | 学科 |
| internship | 实习 | volunteer | 志愿者 |

## In – class Learning

### Skill Tips

*What's a resume?*

- A combination of your education, employment experience, skills and your extra curricular activities.
- It's a marketing document.
- Promote you to a recruiter or prospective employer.
- It's mainly prepared to gain an invitation for a job interview.

*A resume mainly cover:*

- Your profile: sex/gender, age, date of birth, nationality/citizenship, marital status.
- Your key skills: achievement, working experience, education background.
- Get access to numerous online resources on job vacancies.

*Tips for resume:*

- Keep your information clear and easy to read.
- Include key competencies from the job vacancy you are responding to.
- Highlight your most relevant and recent information early in your resume.

### Reading Text

Write Your Cover Letter

*Purpose of Your Cover Letter*

Your cover letter is an important component of the application process. It serves as a way for you to summarize your qualifications, state your interest in a position, and stand out from other applicants. It is specific to each opportunity you are pursuing.

Cover letters should be well written and always accompanied by each resume you send out unless otherwise specified. It is particularly important to include a cover letter, if an objective is not listed on your resume, to be clear on what position you are interested in.

*Tips for Writing Your Cover Letter*

Focus your efforts and include content that is concise, relevant, and appealing to potential employers.

*Be purposeful*

- While every cover letter is different, effective cover letters demonstrate you are a good fit for the position.
- Convey your enthusiasm for the position and knowledge of the company.
- Provide support and examples that showcase the skills and competencies that are being sought.
- Focus on your accomplishments and measurable results.

*Follow standard business writing protocol*

- Address your cover letter to a specific person whenever possible.
- Write clearly and concisely.
- Use proper grammar and check for misspelled words.
- Limit your letter to one page.
- Be sure to include the date, an appropriate salutation, and a closure with your signature.

*Do not mass produce*

- Be sure to relate your specific skills and experiences to each individual position.
- Incorporate information that reflects your knowledge of the company, the industry, or the position.
- Consider that employers are seeking to fill specific roles and are looking for applicants that have the skills and qualities to succeed in that role.

*Structuring Your Cover Letter*

*Paragraph 1: Capture Attention*

- Indicate the position you are applying for and how you learned of the vacancy.
- Outline the specific reasons why you are ideal for the position.
- Sell yourself in paragraph 1.

*Paragraph 2 & 3*: *Create Desire*

- Describe yourself as a serious candidate and one worth inviting for an interview.
- Show, don't tell. Remember, your goal is to set yourself apart from other applicants.
- Emphasize how your variety of experiences are connected to the position and will benefit the company.

*Paragraph 4*: *Call for Action*

- Use a few lines to express your strong interest in the position and your desire to discuss your application further in an interview.

(adapted from https://www.careercenter.illinois.edu/instructable/write-your-cover-letter)

Question 1: Should your cover letter include all the information about you?

Question 2: From the text, what is the proper length of the cover letter?

Question 3: In which paragraph should you sell yourself?

Question 4: In which paragraph should you express your desire for interview?

## Project

Let us write a job application.

Step 1: Read the following job advertisement and answer the questions below.

JOB OPPORTUNITY

ADMINISTRATIVE ASSISTANT

**Responsibilities**:

- To comply with the necessary procedures and controls for the duties and activities within the office including drafting letters, emails, call handling, preparation of correspondences with locals as well as foreigners.

**Requirements**:

- Must have a university degree
- Good command of English language (Reading/Writing)
- High achiever in IELTS or TOEFL will be preferred
- Computer literate, well versed in MS Office and drafting business letters/emails
- Age not more than 45

Email your CV along with Photograph: careerfuture786@gmail.com
only shortlisted candidate will be contacted

Tick or cross the following statements according the advertisement above.

1. If you are not skilled at office software, you are not suit for this job. __________

2. You don't have to speak English in this job. __________

3. This job doesn't ask for writing skills. __________

4. This job doesn't have age limit. __________

Step 2: Suppose you are interested in this position and plan to apply for it. Please write a job application. Try to explain why you are the right person for this job.

## 3. Job Interview

**Pre – class Learning:** Watch the video and learn how to prepare for a job interview, then finish the following tasks.

**Topic:** Think about it and share your opinions on the online forum.

1. What preparations will you do for your job interview?
   (cues: formal clothing, hair style, makeup, resume, copy of certificates and qualifications, etc.)
2. What skills do you think are important for a group interview?
   (cues: confidence, good communication skill, good listener, team spirit, outstanding creation and innovation, etc.)

**Test:** Please watch the video online and answer the questions in the form.

| Please answer the following questions according to what you have learned from the video. |
|---|
| 1. How many types of interview are introduced in the video? |
| 2. Is it true that telephone interview belongs to screen interview? |
| 3. What is recommended after telephone interview? |
| 4. What preparation should you do before a job interview? |

### Wordlist

Glossary

| | | | |
|---|---|---|---|
| trait | 品质 | screen | 屏幕 |
| professional | 专业的 | corporate culture | 企业文化 |
| interviewer | 面试官 | case study | 案例研究 |
| formal | 正式的 | appoint | 约定 |
| voice mail | 语音信箱 | harmony | 和谐 |
| enthusiasm | 热情 | video | 视频 |
| background | 背景 | concise | 简洁的 |

## In – class Learning

### Skill Tips

*Useful expressions at job interview*:

*Ask for job vacancy*

- Do you have any job openings?
- What job vacancy do you have?
- Are you recruiting any people now?
- Are you in need of any staff?

*Ask for information about education background*

- Do you hold a Master's/Bachelor's Degree?
- What kind of certificates do you have?
- Have you got any qualifications?
- Do you have any plans for further education?

*Ask for working experience*

- Do you have any working experience before?
- Is it a full – time or part – time experience?
- How long was your previous job?
- Why did you quit your previous job?

*Discuss about salary and other benefits*:

- How much is your expected salary?
- Does our company offer any other welfare for newcomers?
- Does our company provide staff with any bonus at the end of a year?
- Do employees get any traffic allowance every month?

## Reading Text

### How to Have a Good Job Interview

If you want better results in your job interviews, prepare to rock. Show the employer why you're an ideal candidate for the job, and land it quickly. Follow these steps for your best interview.

1. *Remain respectful, professional and confident, smiling a little*

Don't act nervous, tapping fingers, wagging your legs or wringing your hands nor sitting stiffly as a statue, but also not flopping around like you're lazy. If you're asked to answer a case (what if...) question, talk through the process you would use, in such a case. Don't be afraid to ask whether your ideas sound thorough enough—you'll be evaluated on your ability to structure your thinking and to share your thoughts well.

2. *Sell yourself*

What are your unique selling points and how can you match your highlights to what they want? Make sure you use plenty of examples as proof of your abilities. Show the interviewer that you can find the positives in your past experiences. Focus on how this really is good/much more suitable for you.

3. *Be inquisitive*

Don't forget to ask your questions. Pay attention as the interviewer answers—you may even want to jot down notes. This is both to prove that you are listening and also to give yourself a way to reflect on the interview later if you end up having to decide between multiple positions.

Don't ask the same questions at every interview. Ask questions that are tailored to the company to show that you've really done your research.

4. *Be polite*

Listen to each question fully before you begin to respond. Never assume that your interviewer has read your CV, but don't treat him or her as though he or she hasn't, either. After the interview, do not forget to send a follow - up thank - you email. These are generally better than handwritten thank - you notes, as they are quicker than snail mail. However, you should be sure that it is well proofread and addressed to the right person and identifying yourself and the matters involved, before you send them.

5. *Be persistent*

Keep interviewing. The more you interview, the better you will become at it. Keep aiming for what is realistic for your goals and background, and you will eventually find what you're looking for.

(adapted from website https://www.wikihow.com/Have-a-Good-Job-Interview)

Question 1: What is inappropriate behaviors when doing an interview?

Question 2: How to prove your abilities?

Question 3: Is it a good idea that you would ask the same questions at every interview?

Question 4: What should you do after interview?

## Project

Let us act a job interview as a group.

Step 1: Each group is made of three roles and individuals should make preparations for a job interview with the following instructions.

| HR director: Make a recruitment advertisement and list job descriptions for the position your company is recruiting. |
| --- |
| ________Wanted |

续表

| Interviewer: List six questions that you want to ask during the interview. |
| --- |
| Question one:<br><br>Question two:<br><br>Question three:<br><br>Question four:<br><br>Question five:<br><br>Question six: |
| Interviewee: Write a self – introduction for the job interview and list three questions that you want to ask in the interview. |
| Self – introduction |
| Question one:<br><br>Question two:<br><br>Question three: |

Step 2: Act out a mock job interview in the class.

Model dialogue

A: Good morning, I am Tom Hunter.

B: Good morning, Tom. Please have a seat.

A: Thank you.

B: Tom, I have got your resume, but I would like to know more about you.

A: Thanks for interesting me.

B: Would you like to tell me about yourself?

A: Sure, I was just graduated from ... (university), majoring in ... (major).

B: Why do you choose our company?

A: As far as I know, your company is one of the leading international consultant corporations. I think working here would give me the best chance to use what I have learned at the university.

B: Good. Do you have any certificates or qualifications related to this position?

A: Yes, I've got CET – 6 for English and have a certificate for computer. I also passed my driving test.

B: Did you take any part – time job during your university?

A: I was a teaching assistant for two semesters in my department. It really brought me lots of real – life skills and experiences. I think this will help me in my future career life.

B: Sounds interesting. We will inform you as soon as we have the results.

A: Thanks for your time. I appreciate it very much.

________________________________________

________________________________________

________________________________________

________________________________________

# 4. Tips of Job Interview

**Pre – class Learning:** Watch the video and learn tips of job interview, then finish the following tasks.

**Topic:** Think about it and share your opinions on the online forum.

1. Will you feel nervous when you go to a job interview? Could you think of ways to relax yourself?
   (cues: practice in advance, do some exercise, listen to music, play online games, read a novel, etc.)
2. Will you apply for a position unrelated with your major? If so, what factors will contribute to your decision?
   (cues: company's reputation, curiosity, good offer, interest, sound welfare system, financial incentives, etc.)

**Test:** Please watch the video online and answer the questions in the form.

Please answer the following questions according to what you have learned from the video.

1. Would you please give some examples of ice – breaking?
2. How to remain positive body language when you're talking with others?
3. Do you need to give a quick reply when asked a question raised by the interviewer?
4. What is the focus of the job interview?

**Wordlist**

Glossary

| | | | |
|---|---|---|---|
| ice – breaking | 破冰 | take a deep breath | 深呼吸 |
| trust | 信任 | honest | 诚实 |
| expectation | 期望 | consultation | 咨询 |
| weakness | 弱点 | field | 领域 |
| director | 主管 | cope with | 处理 |

| head office | 总部 | strength | 长处 |
| --- | --- | --- | --- |
| notify | 通知 | probation | 实习 |

## In – class Learning

### Skill Tips

*How to get a job without working experience*

- Showcase your ambition.
- Highlight your soft skills.
- Target your professional network.
- Know the jargon.

### Reading Text

Steps to an Effective Career Plan

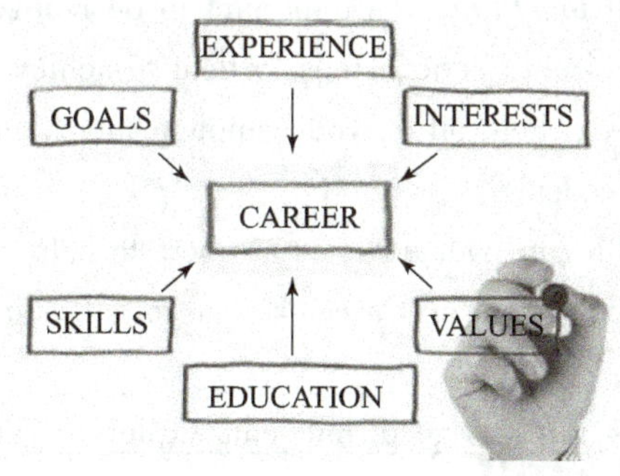


1. *Identify Your Career Options*. Develop a refined list of career options by examining your interests, skills, and values through self – assessment. Narrow your career options by reviewing career information, researching companies, and talking to professionals in the field. You can further narrow your list when you take part in experiences such as volunteering, and internships.

2. *Prioritize*. It's not enough to list options. You have to prioritize. What are your top skills? What interests you the most? What's most important to you? Whether it's challenging work, family – friendly benefits, or the right location, it helps to know what matters to you.

3. *Make Comparisons*. Compare your most promising career options against your list of prioritized skills, interests and values.

4. *Consider Other Factors*. You should consider factors beyond personal preferences. What is the current demand for this field? If the demand is low or entry is diffi-

cult, are you comfortable with risk? What qualifications are required to enter the field? Gather advice from friends, colleagues, and family members.

5. *Make a Choice*. Choose the career paths that are best for you. How many paths you choose depends upon your situation and comfort level. If you're early in your planning, then identifying multiple options may be best. Conversely, narrowing to one or two options may better focus your job search or graduate school applications.

6. *Set "SMART" Goals*. Now that you've identified your career options, develop an action plan to implement this decision. Identify specific, time - bound goals and steps to accomplish your plan. Set short - term goals (to be achieved in one year or less) and long - term goals (to be achieved in one to five years).

- Specific—Identify your goal clearly and specifically.
- Measureable—Include clear criteria to determine progress and accomplishment.
- Attainable—The goal should have a 50 percent or greater chance of success.
- Relevant—The goal is important and relevant to you.
- Time bound—Commit to a specific timeframe.

7. *Create Your Career Action Plan*. It's important to be realistic about expectations and timelines. Write down specific action steps to take to achieve your goals and help yourself stay organized. Check them off as you complete them, but feel free to amend your career action plan as needed.

8. *Meet with a Career Advisor*. Our advisors are here to help you make effective career decisions. Make an appointment on Career Bridge to talk about your career options and concerns.

(adapted from websites https://gecd.mit.edu/explore - careers/career - first - steps/make - career - plan)

Question 1: How to narrow your career options?

Question 2: Why do you prioritize?

Question 3: What are smart goals?

Question 4: Could your career action plan be changeable?

**Project**

Let us do a five - year career plan.

Step 1: What is your expectation of future career? Do you have blue print of your future career? If you don't have a future plan, do you have a short - term goal?

Step 2: Write down your five - year career plan and then share it in the classroom.

Step 3: Analyze whether it is an effective career plan according to what we have learned from the reading material above.

My five – year career plan

(cues: academic life, professional skills, working experience, etc.)

# 5. Job Etiquette

**Pre - class Learning**: Watch the video and learn tips for job etiquette, then finish the following tasks.

**Topic**: Think about it and share your opinions on the online forum.

1. What is office etiquette?
   (cues: formal clothing, respect others' privacy , punctuality, etc.)
2. What is the importance of job etiquette?
   (cues: good relationship with colleagues, harmonious environment, etc.)

**Test**: Please watch the video online and answer the questions in the form.

| Please answer the following questions according to what you have learned from the video. |
|---|
| 1. What should you do if you are found to have some faults in the interview? |
| 2. What should you do if you are faced with conflicts in your workplace? |
| 3. What is the good time for you to network with your colleagues? |

**Wordlist**

Glossary

| co - worker | 同事 | presentation | 陈述 |
|---|---|---|---|
| offend | 冒犯 | conduct | 行为 |

## In - class Learning

### Skill Tips

*Something you have to know in the office*

- Be punctual
- Respect other people's privacy
- Don't gossip or complain
- Don't disturb others

- Be neat and clean
- Be polite to everyone
- Be considerate

## Reading Text

### 3 Essential Office Etiquette Tips

Quite simply, proper office etiquette refers to an unwritten code employees should follow in order to be successful in the workplace. It's a set of norms widely accepted as appropriate behavior.

Here are a few tips for good office etiquette:

1. Dress Appropriately

If the dress code is business casual, make sure you clarify what is and isn't appropriate. Business casual has become the norm for many employers, but many people are still unclear on what this means. For someone, it means polo shirts, casual pants, casual dresses, and so on. Some companies have a business casual policy that excludes jeans or open – toed shoes. Some companies have one dress code when you're working in the office and another when you're meeting with clients.

2. "Please" and "Thank You" Are Still Magic Words

When we were children, "please" and "thank you" were referred to as "magic words" that were to be used when we were asking for something and then, in turn, receiving something. Although we've all outgrown the reminders from our parents, these words have certainly not lost their enchantment. By using common courtesies, you demonstrate you respect the people with whom you're dealing.

3. Be a Team Player

In many workplaces and career fields, it's sometimes tough to get along with varying personalities and that's precisely why clear communication is so important. Part of office etiquette is working well with others and communicating effectively. Take time to listen to other people's points of view. You may not always agree, but it's likely you can learn something new by being open to other perspectives and respectful of other people's opinions. Here are a few additional office etiquette tips to encourage positive working relationships:

- Be friendly and encouraging to co - workers.
- Be responsible—if you say you're going to do something, do it. If you're unable to complete a task for some reason, make sure information is communicated to all team members who would be impacted.
- If you share an office, be considerate. Find out how your office mate works and be respectful. For example, some people need to work in complete silence, while others enjoy background music. Make sure you're not making your office mate crazy with your personal habits.
- Communicate, communicate, and communicate! Your co - workers are not mind readers, so make sure you're communicating with them and your manager on a regular basis.

Proper office etiquette isn't hard to learn, but it's a skill you should constantly practice and improve upon throughout your entire career.

(adapted from https://www.workitdaily.com/office-etiquette-tips)

Question 1: Do all companies have the same dress code for employees?

Question 2: Do "please" and "thank you" words lose their enchantment after we grow up?

Question 3: How to get along with varying personalities in the company?

Question 4: What is the benefit of listening to other people's points of view?

**Project**

Let us talk about office etiquette in a mock office tour.

Step 1: Let us review the office etiquette as a group, then write them down on your notebook.

Step 2: Imagine you are showing two trainees around the company where you work. Explain what different people and departments do. You may use the following pattern:

This is the personnel department.
The personnel manager is the person who...
Here is something you should pay attention to...
Do...
Do not ...

Personnel

- Pays the employees, send staff on training courses

Production

- Production workers: make the products
- Quality controllers: check that the products reach the standards required

Marketing

- Marketing research staff: find out what the market wants
- Marketing planners: decide which new products are needed

Sales

- Sales staff: sell the company's products
- Publicity staff: arrange advertising campaigns

Distribution

- Distribution staff: get the products to the customers

R&D

- Product designers: develop new products

Finance

- Accounts: controls the company's costs
- Bookkeeping: sends out bills to customers

Purchasing

- Purchasing staff: buy raw materials

# Key Reference 参考答案

## Unit 1

### 1. The Overview of Oversea College

Test:

1. 4 years.  2. No.  3. Community college, short – term training.  4. Yes.

Reading Text:

1. They study abroad in the country of their family's origin.

2. By interacting with locals.

3. If you are less outgoing or you never spend much time far from home.

4. Once you become used to a foreign environment, your home might actually seem foreign to you.

### 2. Orientation Week

Test:

1. Orientation week usually refers to the first week which orients your future college life.

2. Usually 7 days, while in the countries, there will be 1 day or 1 month.

3. Attend faculty or school welcome, register information sessions, access online system, sort out student card, connect to Wi – Fi, check out all details (course, personal information), locate support services, remember campus security.

4. Call the emergency phone number or ask for security escort, some universities have shuttle bus for your safety.

Reading Text:

1. Students have the opportunity to travel overseas for week – long, life – changing trips.

2. Students may use the experience to broaden their cultural experiences and overcome anxieties, while making lifelong friends.

3. They can use club – sponsored fundraisers to help offset travel expenses.

4. Club presidents Erin Willis and Erin Grabosky, as well as Associate Director Sheila Marsh.

**3. College Website**

Test:

1. 144.

2. School of Architecture, Design and Planning.

3. No, it doesn't.

Reading Text:

1. No.

2. Colleges offer students many kinds of help making this transition, such as tutoring and academic advising as well as counselling and other support.

3. You get the opportunity to explore.

4. Yes, they do.

**4. On – campus Accommodation**

Test:

1. 先到先得 2. 带公用浴室的单人房 3. 自己煮饭 4. 居住者 5. 不限流量 6. 日常房屋打扫 7. 自习室

Reading Text:

1. Residential advisers and live – in staff members.

2. No, you can apply for university residence halls all year around.

3. No, it doesn't.

4. Making friends. Living on campus provides a great chance to conquer culture barriers.

**5. Write an Enquiry Letter**

Test:

1. Ask information of homestay and the transport.

2. 3 parts: self – introduction, questions, ending.

Reading text:

1. Email.

2. Email is not an immediate method of communication, and you cannot get a more personal response to your enquiry.

3. You'd better prepare a pen and paper to write down information.

4. Online contact forms ensure that you provide all the relevant information about yourself along with your question.

**6. Make an Enquiry Call**

Test:

1. Introduce yourself.

2. Please hold the line please, I will transfer you to .../Hang on please, I will connect you to...

3. Prepare a paper and a pen handy.

4. Pay attention to the time when you make a phone call (time zone, office hour).

Reading Text:

1. Yes, it is.

2. British English.

3. Yes, it is.

4. I'll put you through .../Can you hold the line? / Can you hold on a moment?

## Unit 2

### 1. Airline Company

Test:

1. Singapore Airline, Qatar Airways, ANA all Nippon Airways, Emirates, Lufthansa, Qantas Airways, etc.

2. Limited in – plane space, self – service, low – cost, pay for service. (参考答案)

3. Yes.

4. Pay extra fee.

Reading Text:

1. 2 bags.

2. Pay for additional baggage charges.

3. Yes.

4. The total weight of these items should not exceed 6 kg.

### 2. Take the Flight

Test:

1. terminal

2. airline desk or check – in counter

3. Drop the luggage

4. Security check

5. Custom desk

6. luggage claim

Reading Text:

1. Passengers may have certain illnesses, health and weight – loss goals, or religious commitments that do not allow them to consume standard airline food.

2. By visiting their websites.

3. A day or two before the date of your departure.

4. You should call your airline to make sure that your request for a special meal will be carried over to the other airplane.

**3. City Transportation Site**

Test:

1. Ten. They are tube, train, light railway, monorail, bus, sightseeing bus, shuttle bus, ferry, taxi, bicycle.

2. By using smart card.

3. . gov . info . uk（国家域名）.

4. Websites, books（主观性答案）.

Reading Text:

1. 12 lines.

2. No, they are free.

3. Oyster Card.

4. Because you may save money and avoid the crowds.

**4. Modes of City Transportation**

Test:

1. $3.01

2. $4.20

3. 30%

Reading text:

1. Buy a bus pass.

2. You can usually purchase a bus pass at the city's public transportation website or office.

3. As most city bus drivers aren't authorized to make change for you.

4. Look at the banner.

**5. Car Rental at Abroad**

Test:

1. more

2. more

3. driver's license; passport

4. Car rental company, car type, rental fee, etc.（主观答案）

Reading Text:

1. These websites allow you to search for car rentals in specific locations and for a

specific time frame.

2. Two well – known sites are CarRentals. com and AutoRentals. com.

3. Some rental car companies will provide you with a discount if you pay for the entire rental up – front.

4. Increase your rental time.

**6. Plan a Route**

Test:

1. Plan your route.

2. train; ferry; bus

Reading Text:

1. Flight numbers, hotels, car rentals, and restaurant reservations.

2. You may be able to witness or experience a cultural event that other travelers don't get to experience.

3. Try and condense your travel information into a single document for easy access while travelling. Keep a printed copy or type the details of your itinerary into a word processing document.

4. Because batteries can die.

## Unit 3

**1. Tourism Website**

Test:

1. 8:30 am; 10:15 pm

2. 30 minutes

3. the entrance of the first floor

4. $ 21

Reading Text:

1. It stands for the turning of the century.

2. 30 minutes.

3. Waterloo station.

4. 10:00 am – 9:30 pm daily

**2. Self – guided Tour**

Test:

1. 6:15 pm; 9:30 am

2. adults only nights; tents available

3. $ 301. 50

Reading Text:

1. Westminster Tour (Royal London Tour).

2. Harry Potter Walking Tour.

3. London – All – in – One Tour.

4. London Graffiti and Street Art Tour.

**3. Guided Tour**

Test:

1. 21.

2. Australia.

3. Yes, they do.

4. You will see all the main sighs of Katoomba, the Three Sisters, the Grand Canyon, take the exciting rides at Scenic World and can visit Featherdale wildlife Park.

Reading Text:

1. An exciting whale watch tour.

2. No.

3. A marine environment so rich in nutrients that it attracts some of the most magnificent creatures with which we share our planet.

4. 1 day.

**4. Book Hotel Room**

Test:

1. Booking, Agoda, etc.

2. On official site, you will have specific information of room types, member card benefit, multiple choice, reasonable price and direct contact with customer service.

3. Double room or twin room.

4. It depends on the package that the price includes.

Reading Text:

1. Yes, it is true.

2. If they haven't booked a higher – price room by the time you arrive.

3. You will have a better chance for an upgrade the next time you stay.

4. You can always suggest they can make it up to you with a room upgrade.

**5. Hotel Service**

Test:

1. Send the email.

2. Because the flight lands at midnight.

3. Yes. 10 dollars for one way.

4. The meaning of the room rate "two points package".

Reading Text:

1. Taxes or resort fees. Or services like Wi – Fi, parking, or the use of the fitness center.

2. If they booked their stay through a travel specialist that works closely with a particular hotel.

3. Hotel's staff.

4. Because it will help a traveler to plan out their days.

**6. Tips of Applying for Visa**

Test:

1. 1

2. 15, Nov. 2006

3. Guangzhou China

4. B1/B2

Reading Text:

1. To show other nations that you are a legal citizen of your particular nation of origin.

2. Ten years.

3. A visa specifies certain reasons why that person will be staying in the country while passports are a form of legitimate identity.

4. To protect the people living in their native countries from foreigners who may be terrorists or illegal immigrants.

## Unit 4

**1. Online Shopping**

Test:

1. Product description, price, stock, seller information, shipping rate, evaluation.

2. Out of stock.

3. Conditional free shipping.

4. Customer review, feedback for the shop owner.

Reading Text:

1. If you subscribe to regular delivery.

2. No, Amazon Prime customers enjoy free shipping on all grocery orders.

3. Fresh Direct.

4. Local Harvest aims to connect people in their local communities with fresh, or-

ganic, farm – to – table produce and goods.

**2. Communicate with the Salesman**

Test:

1. Order number, shipping address, payment method, amount, order status.

2. Submit your personal information.

3. You may return or replace goods.

Reading Text:

1. Within 30 days of receipt of the goods.

2. You may be offered a partial refund or repair, depending on the product and usage.

3. Notify the Customer Service within 48 hours.

4. You can escalate your complaint.

**3. Tips of Money Saving**

Test:

1. Yard sale, church sale, garage sale, outdoor fair, market, consignment store.

2. You have early access to the lightening deal.

3. No.

4. Great value product.

Reading Text:

1. Yes.

2. Show some interest in an item but say, "It's just too much money." If he comes down even 2 percent, there's nothing sacred about the price tag.

3. No, it is not true.

4. No, you'll never get the best price.

**4. Order Fast Food**

Test:

1. A drive – through restaurant.

2. Mac veggie.

3. Chicken burger meal includes drinks and extra snacks.

4. Four.

Reading Text:

1. In 1916.

2. Burgers and fries.

3. Yes, it has embraced ethnic food.

4. It is often reserved for special occasions.

### 5. Eat at Restaurant

Test:

1. American style and European style.

2. American style of dinning.

3. When people have the beverage and the bite of bread.

Reading Text:

1. Group.

2. What would you recommend? /What are the specialities? /What are today's specials?

3. You can use the waiter's expert knowledge to help choose something great.

4. Usually 10% -15% of the bill.

### 6. Oversea Supermarket

Test:

1. Grain bread.

2. Free range egg.

3. Gluten free food.

Reading Text:

1. Making changes to your diet.

2. Fiber takes your body longer to digest, also improves bowel function, preventing constipation.

3. Soy milk, tofu, and salmon with the bones and broccoli.

4. No, it is not true.

## Unit 5

### 1. Find a Job Abroad

Test:

1. A circle of friend, newspaper, website.

2. Online resources, career consultancy, workshop, bulletin board.

3. What and Where.

Reading Text:

1. Transferable skills.

2. Interpersonal and self - directional skills.

3. Across - job skills/Transferable skills.

4. "Why should I hire you?"

**2. Application Letter and Resume**

Test:

1. Cover letter, resume, selection criteria.

2. It introduces your application and reasons for applying for the job, linking the relevant skills and experience on your resume to the job requirements and organization.

3. No.

4. The aim of selection criteria is to provide more details about how you have demonstrated the competencies required to do the job.

Reading Text:

1. No, it shouldn't.

2. Limit your letter to one page.

3. Paragraph 1.

4. Paragraph 4.

**3. Job Interview**

Test:

1. 5.

2. Yes, it is.

3. Sending a letter to say thanks.

4. Self – assessment.

Reading Text:

1. Act nervous, tapping fingers, wagging your legs or wringing your hands, sitting stiffly as a statue, and flopping around like you're lazy.

2. Use plenty of examples.

3. No, it isn't.

4. Sending a follow – up thank – you email.

**4. Tips of Job Interview**

Test:

1. Ask some warm – up questions like the latest news of the company.

2. Keep eye contact, smile.

3. No, you don't have to.

4. Why you are the right person for this position.

Reading Text:

1. By reviewing career information, researching companies, and talking to professionals in the field.

2. Because it helps to know what matters to you.

3. Smart goals are specific, time – bound goals.

4. Yes, it could be changeable.

**5. Job Etiquette**

Test:

1. Admit it and change the subject quickly.

2. Be sure to handle them in the most professional manner.

3. Lunch time.

Reading Text:

1. No, they don't.

2. No, they don't.

3. Clear communication.

4. It's likely you can learn something new by being open to other perspectives and respectful of other people's opinions.